101
Stitches for Afghans

Bobbie Matela, Managing Editor
Carol Wilson Mansfield, Art Director
Mary Ann Frits, Editorial Director
Kathy Wesley, Pattern Editor
Ann Kirtley, Technical Editor
Graphic Solutions, inc-chgo, Book Design

For a full-color catalogue including books of crochet designs, write to:

American School of Needlework®, Consumer Division
1455 Linda Vista Drive, San Marcos, CA 92069

Patterns tested and models made by Mary Ann Frits, Tammy Hebert,
Pat Hyland, Melody Long, Dolores Roberts, Kelly Robinson,
Landee Roth and Sandy Scoville.

We have made every effort to ensure the accuracy and completeness
of these instructions. We cannot, however, be responsible for human
error, typographical mistakes, or variations in individual work.

Introduction

More afghans are crocheted each year than any other single crochet project. Afghans are fun to make, cozy to use, and make wonderful gifts.

Afghan addicts will love the stitch patterns in this book. We've carefully chosen them so that they're not too open (who wants to catch a toe in an afghan?), not too difficult, and not too time-consuming.

This book is a reference tool you will use for years; you can crochet the stitch patterns in worsted or bulky yarn, in baby or sport weight, in your own choice of colors.

Before You Begin

Unlike most crochet patterns, those in this book specify no gauge, no material requirements, and no hook sizes.

That is because each stitch can be worked in your choice of yarn to vary the size and appearance of each stitch to fit your project.

The actual-size photos here and on page 5 show stitch pattern #59 worked in four different weights of yarn and four different hook sizes. You can see how the yarn will change the look of the stitch.

When choosing the material and hook for your project, you may wish to do some experimenting with a variety of materials until you achieve the appearance and texture that pleases you.

The stitch patterns photographed throughout this book were all made with worsted weight yarn and a size I aluminum hook.

Baby weight yarn with E hook

Multiples

A multiple is the number of chains required for each repeat of the stitch pattern; to this we may then add a specified number of chains to make the pattern end correctly.

If a pattern specifies a multiple of 6 + 2, for example, you need to make a starting chain in multiples of 6 (12, 18, 24, etc): then add a final 2 chains. The number of chains given after the + sign in a multiple is added only once.

Helpful Hint: *When working a long foundation chain, add a few extra chains to ensure that the first row of the pattern will not run out of chains; then at the end of the first row, rip out any extra chains.*

Sport weight yarn with F hook

Worsted weight yarn with I hook

Bulky weight yarn with J hook

Abbreviations & Symbols

beg .... begin(ning)

BL(s) .... back loop(s)

BPdc .... back post double crochet(s)

BPsc .... back post single crochet(s)

ch(s) .... chain(s)

CL(s) .... cluster(s)

dc .... double crochet(s)

dec .... decrease(-ing)

dtrc .... double triple crochet(s)

FL(s) .... front loop(s)

FPdc .... front post double crochet(s)

FPdtrc .... front post double triple crochet(s)

FPsc .... front post single crochet(s)

FPtr trc .... front post triple triple crochet(s)

hdc .... half double crochet(s)

lp(s) .... loop(s)

patt .... pattern

PC(s) .... popcorn(s)

prev .... previous

rem .... remain(ing)

rep .... repeat(ing)

rev .... reverse

rnd(s) .... round(s)

sc .... single crochet(s)

sk .... skip

sl .... slip

sl st(s) .... slip stitch(es)

sp(s) .... space(s)

st(s) .... stitch(es)

tog .... together

tr trc .... triple triple crochet(s)

trc .... triple crochet(s)

YO .... yarn over

* An asterisk is used to mark the beginning of a portion of instructions to be worked more than once; thus, "rep from ***** twice more" means after working the instructions once, repeat the instructions following the asterisk twice more (3 times in all).

† The dagger identifies a portion of instructions that will be repeated again later in the same row or round.

— The number after a long dash at the end of a row or round indicates the number of stitches you should have when the row or round has been completed. The long dash can also be used to indicate a completed stitch such as a decrease, a shell, or a cluster.

( ) Parentheses are used to enclose instructions which should be worked the exact number of times specified immediately following the parentheses, such as "(2 sc in next dc, sc in next dc) twice." They are also used to set off and clarify a group of stitches that are to be worked all into the same space or stitch, such as "(2 dc, ch 1, 2 dc) in corner sp."

[ ] Brackets and **( )** parentheses are used to provide additional information to clarify instructions.
Join - join with a sl st unless otherwise specified.

The patterns in this book are written using United States terminology. Terms which have different English equivalents are noted below.

United States	English
single crochet (sc) .... double crochet (dc)
half double crochet (hdc) .... half treble (htr)
double crochet (dc) .... treble (tr)
triple crochet (trc) .... double treble (dtr)
double triple crochet (dtrc) .... triple treble (trtr)
triple triple crochet (tr trc) .... quadruple treble (q[uad]tr)
skip (sk) .... miss
slip stitch (sl st) .... slip stitch (ss) or "single crochet"
gauge .... tension
yarn over (YO) .... yarn over hook (YOH)

Stitch Guide

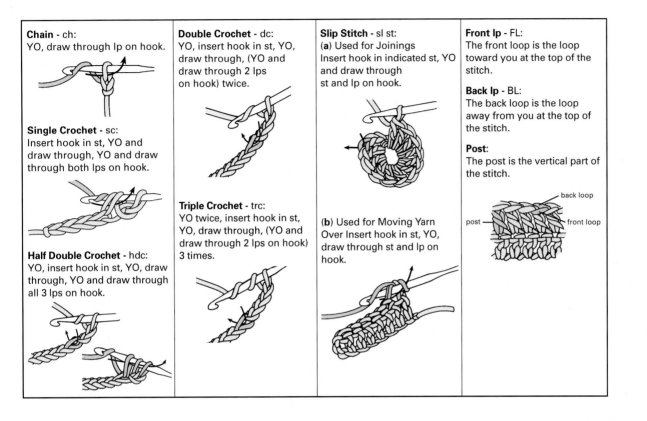

Chain - ch:
YO, draw through lp on hook.

Single Crochet - sc:
Insert hook in st, YO and draw through, YO and draw through both lps on hook.

Half Double Crochet - hdc:
YO, insert hook in st, YO, draw through, YO and draw through all 3 lps on hook.

Double Crochet - dc:
YO, insert hook in st, YO, draw through, (YO and draw through 2 lps on hook) twice.

Triple Crochet - trc:
YO twice, insert hook in st, YO, draw through, (YO and draw through 2 lps on hook) 3 times.

Slip Stitch - sl st:
(**a**) Used for Joinings
Insert hook in indicated st, YO and draw through st and lp on hook.

(**b**) Used for Moving Yarn Over Insert hook in st, YO, draw through st and lp on hook.

Front lp - FL:
The front loop is the loop toward you at the top of the stitch.

Back lp - BL:
The back loop is the loop away from you at the top of the stitch.

Post:
The post is the vertical part of the stitch.

Metric Conversion Charts

INCHES INTO MILLIMETERS & CENTIMETERS (Rounded off slightly)

inches	mm	cm	inches	cm	inches	cm	inches	cm
1/8	3		5	12.5	21	53.5	38	96.5
1/4	6		5 1/2	14	22	56	39	99
3/8	10	1	6	15	23	58.5	40	101.5
1/2	13	1.3	7	18	24	61	41	104
5/8	15	1.5	8	20.5	25	63.5	42	106.5
3/4	20	2	9	23	26	66	43	109
7/8	22	2.2	10	25.5	27	68.5	44	112
1	25	2.5	11	28	28	71	45	114.5
1 1/4	32	3.2	12	30.5	29	73.5	46	117
1 1/2	38	3.8	13	33	30	76	47	119.5
1 3/4	45	4.5	14	35.5	31	79	48	122
2	50	5	15	38	32	81.5	49	124.5
2 1/2	65	6.5	16	40.5	33	84	50	127
3	75	7.5	17	43	34	86.5		
3 1/2	90	9	18	46	35	89		
4	100	10	19	48.5	36	91.5		
4 1/2	115	11.5	20	51	37	94		

mm - millimeter   cm - centimeter

CROCHET HOOKS CONVERSION CHART

U.S.	1/B	2/C	3/D	4/E	5/F	6/G	8/H	9/I	10/J	10 1/2/K
English	12	11	10	9	8	7	6	5	4	2
Continental-mm	2.25	2.75	3.25	3.5	3.75	4.25	5	5.5	6	6.5

#1

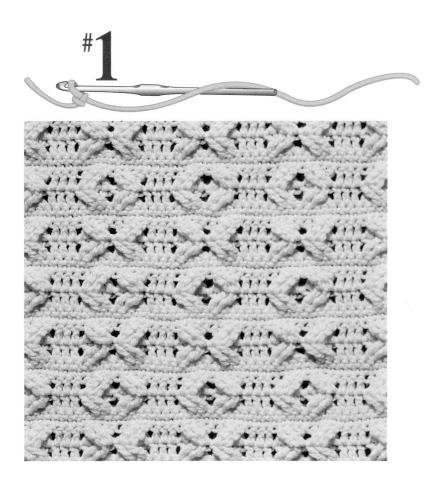

Materials:

Yarn—One color

Instructions

Foundation ch: multiple of 11 + 4

Row 1 (right side):
Sc in 2nd ch from hook and in each rem ch. Ch 1, turn.

Row 2:
Sc in each sc. Ch 2 (counts as first dc on following rows), turn.

Row 3:
Dc in next 2 sc; * sk next 2 sc, trc in next 2 sc, working behind trc just made, trc in each skipped sc; sk next 2 sc, trc in next 2 sc; working in front of trc just made, trc in each skipped sc; dc in next 3 sc; rep from * across. Ch 2, turn.

Row 4:
Dc in next 2 dc; * sk next 2 trc, trc in next 2 trc, working behind trc just made, trc in each skipped trc; sk next 2 trc, trc in next 2 trc; working in front of trc just made, trc in each skipped trc; dc in next 3 dc; rep from * across, ending with last dc in 2nd ch of turning ch-2. Ch 1, turn.

Row 5:
Sc in each st to turning ch-2; sc in 2nd ch of turning ch-2. Ch 1, turn.

Row 6:
Sc in each sc. Ch 2, turn.

Row 7:
Dc in next 2 sc; * sk next 2 sc, trc in next 2 sc, working in front of trc just made, trc in each skipped sc; sk next 2 sc, trc in next 2 sc; working behind trc just made, trc in each skipped sc; dc in next 3 sc; rep from * across. Ch 2, turn.

Row 8:
Dc in next 2 dc; * sk next 2 trc, trc in next 2 trc, working in front of trc just made, trc in each skipped trc; sk next 2 trc, trc in next 2 trc; working behind trc just made, trc in each skipped trc; dc in next 3 dc; rep from * across, ending with last dc in 2nd ch of turning ch-2. Ch 1, turn.

Rows 9 and 10:
Rep Rows 5 and 6.

Rep Rows 3 through 10 for desired length, ending with Row 6. At end of last row, do not ch 2; do not turn.

Finish off.

#2

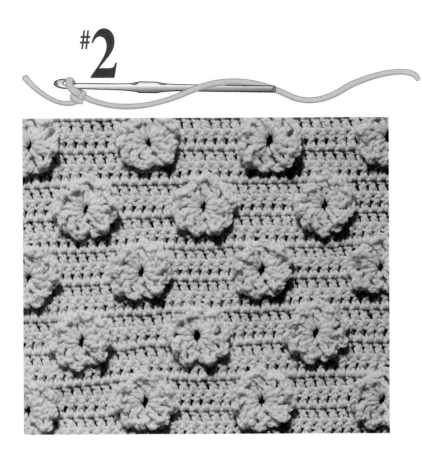

Materials:
Yarn—One color

Pattern Stitches

Front Post Double Crochet (FPdc):
YO, insert hook from front to back to front around post **(**see page 7**)** of next dc, draw up lp, **(**YO, draw through 2 lps on hook**)** twice—FPdc made.

Circle:
Work **(**FPdc, ch 3**)** around next dc; work **(**FPdc, ch 3**)** 5 times around same dc; turn piece upside down, work **(**FPdc, ch 3**)** 5 times around prev dc on same row, dc around same post—circle made.
Note: When completing row, work behind circle in same dc as post worked for beg of circle.

Instructions
Foundation ch: multiple of 12 + 1

Row 1 (wrong side):
Dc in 3rd ch from hook (2 skipped chs count as a dc) and in each rem ch. Ch 2 (counts as first dc on following rows), turn.

Row 2 (right side):
Dc in each dc to beg 2 skipped chs; dc in 2nd ch of beg 2 skipped chs. Ch 2, turn.

Row 3:
Dc in each dc to turning ch-2; dc in 2nd ch of turning ch-2. Ch 2, turn.

Row 4:
Dc in next 5 dc, circle (see Pattern Stitch); * dc behind same dc as beg of circle and in next 11 dc, circle; rep from * to last 6 sts; dc in next 5 dc and in 2nd ch of turning ch-2. Ch 2, turn.

Row 5:
Dc in next 5 dc, sk next circle; * dc in next 12 dc, sk next circle; rep from * to last 6 sts; dc in next 5 dc and in 2nd ch of turning ch-2. Ch 2, turn.

Rows 6 and 7:
Rep Row 3.

Row 8:
Dc in next 11 dc, circle; * dc behind same dc as beg of circle and in next 11 dc, circle; rep from * to last 12 sts; dc in next 11 dc and in 2nd ch of turning ch-2. Ch 2, turn.

Row 9:
Dc in next 11 dc, sk next circle; * dc in next 12 dc, sk next circle; rep from * to last 12 sts; dc in next 11 dc and in 2nd ch of turning ch-2. Ch 2, turn.

Rows 10 and 11:
Rep Row 3.

Rep Rows 4 through 11 for desired length, ending with Row 5. At end of last row, do not ch 2; do not turn.

Finish off.

#3

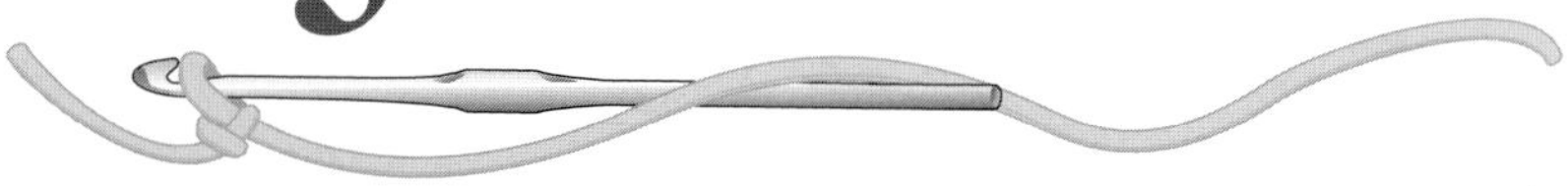

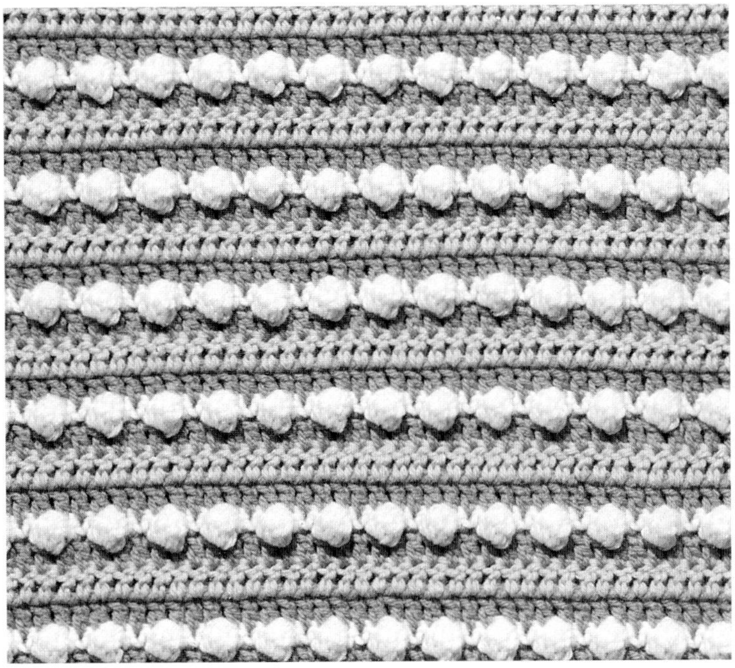

Materials:
Yarn—Color A (light); Color B (dark);
  Color C (off white)

Pattern Stitch

Cluster (CL):
Keeping last lp of each dc on hook, 4 dc in st
indicated; YO and draw through all 5 lps on hook—
CL made. Push CL to right side.

Instructions
Foundation ch with Color A: multiple of 3

Row 1 (wrong side):
Dc in 3rd ch from hook (2 skipped chs count as a dc)
and in each rem ch; change to Color B by drawing lp
through; cut Color A. Ch 2 (counts as first dc on
following rows), turn.

Row 2 (right side):
Dc in each dc to beg 2 skipped chs; dc in 2nd ch of beg
2 skipped chs; change to Color C by drawing lp
through; cut Color B. Ch 1, turn.

Row 3:
Sc in first 2 dc; * CL (see Pattern Stitch) in next dc;
sc in next 2 dc; rep from * across, working last sc in
2nd ch of turning ch-2; change to Color B by drawing
lp through; cut Color C. Ch 2, turn.

Row 4:
Dc in each sc and in each CL; change to Color A by
drawing lp through; cut Color B. Ch 2, turn.

Row 5:
Dc in each dc to turning ch-2; dc in 2nd ch of turning
ch-2; change to Color B by drawing lp through; cut
Color A. Ch 2, turn.

Row 6:
Dc in each dc to turning ch-2; dc in 2nd ch of turning
ch-2; change to Color C by drawing lp through; cut
Color B. Ch 1, turn.

Rep Rows 3 through 6 for desired length, ending with
Row 5. At end of last row, do not ch 2; do not turn.

Finish off.

#4

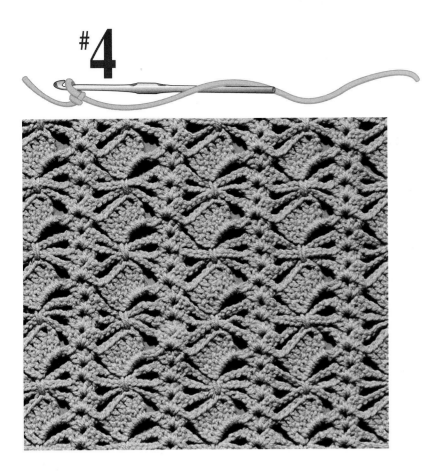

Materials:
Yarn—One color

Instructions
Foundation ch: multiple of 10

Row 1 (wrong side):
Hdc in 3rd ch from hook **(2 skipped chs count as an hdc)** and in each rem ch. Ch 2 **(counts as first dc on following rows)**, turn.

Row 2 (right side):
Dc in next hdc, sk next 2 hdc; * in next hdc work **(2 dc, ch 2, 2 dc)—V-st made;** ch 5, sk next 4 hdc, sc in next hdc, ch 3, turn; 5 dc in ch-5 sp, ch 3, turn; dc in next 4 dc and in 3rd ch of turning ch-3—dc square made; on working row, sk next 4 hdc; rep from * to last 5 sts; in next hdc work **(2 dc, ch 2, 2 dc)—V-st made;** sk next 2 hdc, dc in next hdc and in 2nd ch of beg 2 skipped chs. Ch 2, turn.

Row 3:
Dc in next dc; * in ch-2 sp of next V-st work V-st; ch 9; rep from * to last V-st; in ch-2 sp of last V-st work V-st; sk next 2 dc of same V-st, dc in next dc and in 2nd ch of turning ch-2. Ch 2, turn.

Rows 4 and 5:
Rep Row 3.

Row 6:
Dc in next dc; * V-st in next V-st; ch 5, working over ch-9 sps of Rows 3, 4 and 5, sc in 3rd ch of turning ch-3 of dc square; ch 3, turn; 5 dc in ch-5 sp, ch 3, turn; dc in next 4 dc and in 3rd ch of turning ch-3—dc square made; rep from * to last V-st; V-st in last V-st; sk next 2 dc of same V-st, dc in next dc and in 2nd ch of turning ch-2. Ch 2, turn.

Rep Rows 3 through 6 for desired length.

Next Row:
Dc in next dc; * V-st in next V-st; ch 4, sk next 2 dc of same V-st and next 5 dc of dc square, sc in 3rd ch of turning ch-3 of dc square; ch 4; rep from * across to last V-st; V-st in last V-st; sk next 2 dc of same V-st, dc in next dc and in 2nd ch of turning ch-2. Ch 2, turn.

Last Row:
Hdc in next dc, in next 2 dc of next V-st, and in next ch-2 sp; * sk next 2 dc of same V-st, hdc in next 4 chs, in next sc, in next 4 chs, and in ch-2 sp of next V-st; rep from * to last 2 dc of last V-st; hdc in last 2 dc of last V-st, in next dc, and in 2nd ch of turning ch-2.

Finish off.

#5

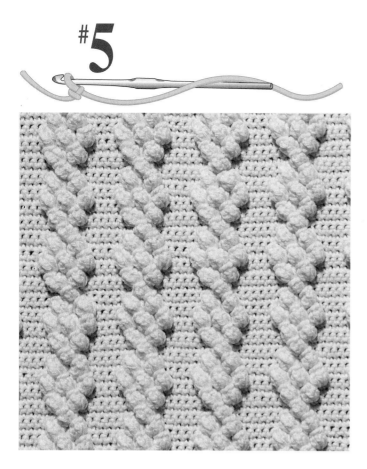

Materials:
Yarn—One color

Pattern Stitch

Popcorn (PC):
5 dc in st indicated; drop lp from hook, insert hook in first dc made, draw dropped lp through; pull tight—PC made.

Instructions
Foundation ch: multiple of 10 + 2

Row 1 (wrong side):
Sc in 2nd ch from hook and in each rem ch. Ch 1, turn.

Row 2 (right side):
Sc in first 5 sc, PC (see Pattern Stitch) in next sc; * sc in next 9 sc, PC in next sc; rep from * to last 5 sc; sc in last 5 sc. Ch 1, turn.

Row 3:
Sc in first 5 sc, ch 1, sk next PC; * sc in next 9 sc, ch 1, sk next PC; rep from * to last 5 sc; sc in last 5 sc. Ch 1, turn.

Row 4:
Sc in first 4 sc, PC in next sc; sc in next ch-1 sp, PC in next sc; * sc in next 7 sc, PC in next sc; sc in next ch-1 sp, PC in next sc; rep from * to last 4 sc; sc in last 4 sc. Ch 1, turn.

Row 5:
Sc in first 4 sc, ch 1, sk next PC, sc in next sc, ch 1, sk next PC; * sc in next 7 sc, ch 1, sk next PC, sc in next sc, ch 1, sk next PC; rep from * to last 4 sc; sc in last 4 sc. Ch 1, turn.

Row 6:
Sc in first 3 sc, (PC in next sc, sc in next ch-1 sp) twice; PC in next sc; * sc in next 5 sc, (PC in next sc, sc in next ch-1 sp) twice; PC in next sc; rep from * to last 3 sc; sc in last 3 sc. Ch 1, turn.

Row 7:
Sc in first 3 sc, (ch 1, sk next PC, sc in next sc) twice; ch 1, sk next PC; * sc in next 5 sc, (ch 1, sk next PC, sc in next sc) twice; ch 1, sk next PC; rep from * to last 3 sc; sc in last 3 sc. Ch 1, turn.

Row 8:
Sc in first 3 sc and in next ch-1 sp, PC in next sc; sc in next ch-1 sp, PC in next sc; * sc in next ch-1 sp, in next 5 sc, and in next ch-1 sp; PC in next sc; sc in next ch-1 sp, PC in next sc; rep from * to last ch-1 sp; sc in last ch-1 sp and in last 3 sc. Ch 1, turn.

Row 9:
Rep Row 5.

Row 10:
Sc in first 4 sc and in next ch-1 sp, PC in next sc; * sc in next ch-1 sp, in next 7 sc, and in next ch-1 sp; PC in next sc; rep from * to last ch-1 sp; sc in last ch-1 sp and in last 4 sc. Ch 1, turn.

Rep Rows 3 through 10 for desired length.

Last Row:
Sc in each sc and in each PC.

Finish off.

#6

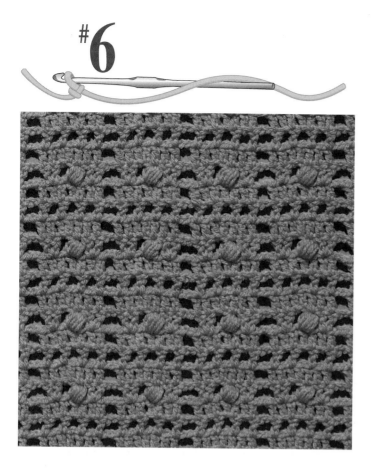

Materials:
Yarn—One color

Pattern Stitch

Puff Stitch (puff st):
(YO, draw up lp in st indicated) 5 times; YO and draw through all 11 lps on hook—puff st made. Push puff st to right side.

Instructions
Foundation ch: multiple of 9 + 7

Row 1 (right side):
Dc in 3rd ch from hook (2 skipped chs count as a dc), ch 2; * sk next 2 chs, dc in next 7 chs, ch 2; rep from * to last 4 chs; sk next 2 chs, dc in next 2 chs. Ch 2 (counts as first dc on following rows), turn.

Row 2:
Dc in next dc, ch 2; * sk next ch-2 sp and next dc; 2 dc in next dc; ch 1, sk next dc, puff st (see Pattern Stitch) in next dc; ch 1, sk next dc, 2 dc in next dc; ch 2, sk next dc; rep from * to last 2 sts; dc in next dc and in 2nd ch of beg 2 skipped chs. Ch 2, turn.

Row 3:
Dc in next dc; * ch 2, sk next ch-2 sp, dc in next 7 sts; rep from * to last ch-2 sp; ch 2, sk last ch-2 sp, dc in next dc and in 2nd ch of turning ch-2. Ch 2, turn.

Row 4:
Dc in next dc; * ch 2, sk next ch-2 sp, dc in next dc, (ch 1, sk next dc, dc in next dc) 3 times; rep from * to last ch-2 sp; ch 2, sk last ch-2 sp, dc in next dc and in 2nd ch of turning ch-2. Ch 2, turn.

Row 5:
Dc in next dc; * ch 2, sk next ch-2 sp, dc in next dc, (dc in next ch and in next dc) 3 times; rep from * to last ch-2 sp; ch 2, sk last ch-2 sp, dc in next dc and in 2nd ch of turning ch-2. Ch 2, turn.

Row 6:
Dc in next dc, ch 2; * sk next ch-2 sp and next dc; 2 dc in next dc; ch 1, sk next dc, puff st in next dc; ch 1, sk next dc, 2 dc in next dc; ch 2, sk next dc; rep from * to last ch-2 sp; ch 2, sk last ch-2 sp, dc in next dc and in 2nd ch of turning ch-2. Ch 2, turn.

Row 7:
Dc in next dc; * ch 2, sk next ch-2 sp, dc in next 7 sts; rep from * to last ch-2 sp; ch 2, sk last ch-2 sp, dc in next dc and in 2nd ch of turning ch-2. Ch 2, turn.

Rep Rows 4 through 7 for desired length. At end of last row, do not ch 2; do not turn.

Finish off.

#7

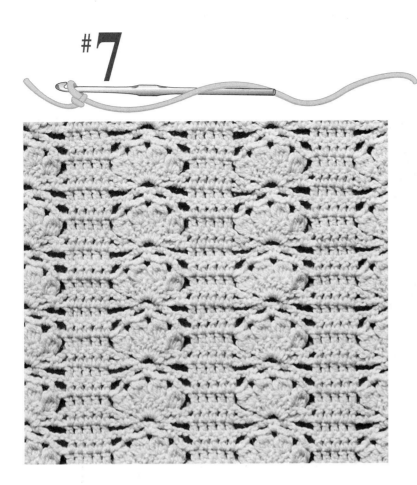

Materials:
Yarn—One color

Pattern Stitch

Cluster (CL):
Keeping last lp of each dc on hook, 4 dc in st indicated; YO and draw through all 5 lps on hook—CL made.

Instructions
Foundation ch: multiple of 16 + 6

Row 1 (right side):
Dc in 3rd ch from hook (2 skipped chs count as a dc) and in next 3 chs; ***** ch 4, sk next 4 chs, sc in next ch, ch 3, sk next ch, sc in next ch, ch 4, sk next 4 chs, dc in next 5 chs; rep from ***** across. Ch 2 (counts as first dc on following rows), turn.

Row 2:
Dc in next 4 dc; ***** ch 2, sc in next ch-4 sp, ch 1, 7 dc in next ch-3 sp; ch 1, sc in next ch-4 sp, ch 2, dc in next 5 dc; rep from ***** across, working last dc in 2nd ch of beg 2 skipped chs. Ch 2, turn.

Row 3:
Dc in next 4 dc; ***** ch 1, sk next sc, CL (see Pattern Stitch) in next dc; (ch 3, sk next dc, CL in next dc) 3 times; ch 1, sk next sc, dc in next 5 dc; rep from ***** across, working last dc in 2nd ch of turning ch-2. Ch 2, turn.

Row 4:
Dc in next 4 dc; ***** ch 2, sk next ch-1 sp, sc in next ch-3 sp, (ch 3, sc in next ch-3 sp) twice; ch 2, sk next CL, dc in next 5 dc; rep from ***** across, working last dc in 2nd ch of turning ch-2. Ch 2, turn.

Row 5:
Dc in next 4 dc; ***** ch 4, sk next ch-2 sp, sc in next ch-3 sp, ch 3, sc in next ch-3 sp, ch 4, dc in next 5 dc; rep from ***** across, working last dc in 2nd ch of turning ch-2. Ch 2, turn.

Rep Rows 2 through 5 for desired length. At end of last row, do not ch 2; do not turn.

Finish off.

#8

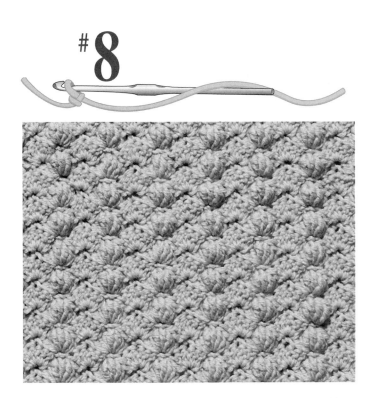

Materials:
Yarn—One color

Instructions
Foundation ch: multiple of 6 + 2

Row 1 (wrong side):
Sc in 2nd ch from hook and in each rem ch. Ch 1, turn.

Row 2 (right side):
Sc in first sc; * sk next 2 sc, in next sc work (2 dc, 3 trc, 2 dc)—shell made; sk next 2 sc, sc in next sc; rep from * across. Ch 2 (counts as first dc on following rows), turn.

Row 3:
2 dc in first sc; sc in BL of 2nd trc of next shell; * 5 dc in next sc; sc in BL of 2nd trc of next shell; rep from * to last sc; 3 dc in last sc. Ch 1, turn.

Row 4:
Sc in first dc; * shell in next sc; sc in 3rd dc of next 5-dc group; rep from * to turning ch-2; sc in 2nd ch of turning ch-2. Ch 2, turn.

Rep Rows 3 and 4 for desired length, ending with Row 3. At end of last row, do not ch 1; do not turn.

Finish off.

#9

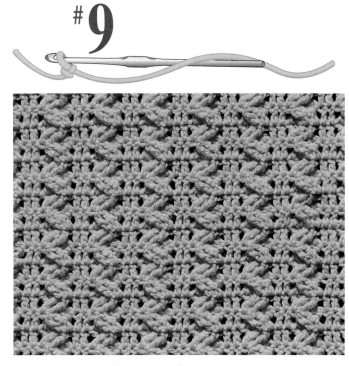

Materials:
Yarn—One color

Instructions
Foundation ch: multiple of 6 + 3

Row 1 (wrong side):
Dc in 3rd ch from hook (2 skipped chs count as a dc) and in each rem ch. Ch 2 (counts as first dc on following rows), turn.

Row 2 (right side):
Dc in next dc; * sk next 2 dc, trc in next 2 dc, working behind 2 trc just made, trc in 2 skipped dc; dc in next 2 dc; rep from * across, working last dc in 2nd ch of beg 2 skipped chs. Ch 2, turn.

Row 3:
Dc in next dc; * sk next 2 trc, trc in next 2 trc, working in front of 2 trc just made, trc in 2 skipped trc; dc in next 2 dc; rep from * across, working last dc in 2nd ch of turning ch-2. Ch 2, turn.

Row 4:
Dc in next dc; * sk next 2 trc, trc in next 2 trc, working behind 2 trc just made, trc in 2 skipped trc; dc in next 2 dc; rep from * across, working last dc in 2nd ch of turning ch-2. Ch 2, turn.

Rep Rows 3 and 4 for desired length.

Last Row:
Dc in next dc and in each trc and dc, working last dc in 2nd ch of turning ch-2.

Finish off.

Materials:
Yarn—Color A (dark); Color B (light)

Color Sequence:
4 rows Color A
4 rows Color B
end with 4 rows Color A

Pattern Stitches

Double Triple Crochet (dtrc):
YO 3 times, draw up lp in st indicated, (YO, draw through 2 lps on hook) 4 times—dtrc made.

Double Triple Crochet Cluster (dtrcCL):
Keeping last lp of each dtrc on hook, 3 dtrc in st indicated; YO and draw through all 4 lps on hook—dtrcCL made.

Instructions
Foundation ch with Color A: multiple of 17 + 16

Row 1 (right side):
Sc in 2nd ch from hook and in next 6 chs, 3 sc in next ch; sc in next 7 chs; * sk next 2 chs, sc in next 7 chs, 3 sc in next ch; sc in next 7 chs; rep from * across. Ch 1, turn.

Row 2:
Sk first sc, working in BLs only, sc in next 7 sc, 3 sc in next sc—3-sc point made; * sc in next 7 sc, sk next 2 sc, sc in next 7 sc, 3 sc in next sc; rep from * to last 8 sc; sc in next 6 sc, sk next sc, sc in last sc. Ch 1, turn.

Row 3:
Rep Row 2.

Row 4:
Rep Row 2. At end of row, change to next color in sequence by drawing lp through; cut prev color. Ch 1, turn.

Row 5:
Sk first sc, working through both lps, sc in next 3 sc; dtrcCL (see Pattern Stitches) in first unused lp of 3-sc point in 3rd row below; on working row, sk next sc, sc in next 3 sc, 3 sc in next sc; sc in next 3 sc, dtrcCL in 3rd unused lp of same 3-sc point on 3rd row below; * on working row, sk next sc, sc in next 3 sc, sk next 2 sc, sc in next 3 sc, dtrcCL in first unused lp of next 3-sc point on 3rd row below; on working row, sk next sc, sc in next 3 sc, 3 sc in next sc; sc in next 3 sc, dtrcCL in 3rd unused lp of same 3-sc point on 3rd row below; rep from * to last 5 sc; on working row, sk next sc, sc in next 2 sc, sk next sc, sc in last sc. Ch 1, turn.

Row 6:
Sk first sc, working in BLs only, sc in next 7 sts, 3 sc in next sc; * sc in next 7 sts, sk next 2 sc, sc in next 7 sts, 3 sc in next sc; rep from * to last 8 sc; sc in next 6 sc, sk next sc, sc in last sc. Ch 1, turn.

Row 7:
Rep Row 2.

Row 8:
Rep Row 2. At end of row, change to next color in sequence by drawing lp through; cut prev color. Ch 1, turn.

Working in color sequence, rep Rows 5 through 8 for desired length. At end of last row, do not ch 1; do not turn.

Finish off.

#11

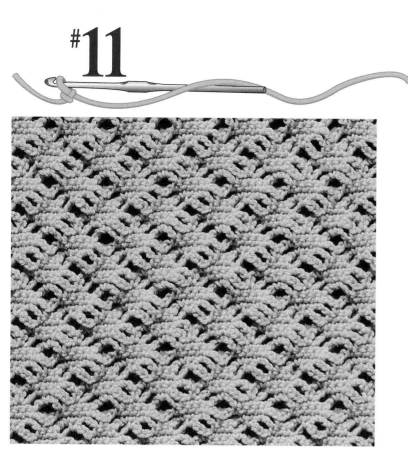

Materials:
Yarn—One color

Instructions
Foundation ch: multiple of 6 + 4

Row 1 (right side):
Sc in 2nd ch from hook and in each rem ch. Ch 1, turn.

Row 2:
Sc in first 4 sc; * ch 5, sk next sc, sc in next 5 sc; rep from * to last 5 sc; ch 5, sk next sc, sc in last 4 sc. Ch 1, turn.

Row 3:
Sc in first 3 sc; * ch 3, sc in next ch-5 sp, ch 3, sk next sc, sc in next 3 sc; rep from * across. Ch 1, turn.

Row 4:
Sc in first 2 sc; * ch 3, sc in next ch-3 sp, in next sc, and in next ch-3 sp; ch 3, sk next sc, sc in next sc; rep from * to last sc; sc in last sc. Ch 2 (counts as first dc on following rows), turn.

Row 5:
Dc in next sc, ch 3, sc in next ch-3 sp, in next 3 sc, and in next ch-3 sp; * ch 5, sc in next ch-3 sp, in next 3 sc, and in next ch-3 sp; rep from * to last 2 sc; ch 3, dc in last 2 sc. Ch 1, turn.

Row 6:
Sc in first 2 dc, ch 3, sk next sc, sc in next 3 sc; * ch 3, sc in next ch-5 sp, ch 3, sk next sc, sc in next 3 sc; rep from * to last ch-3 sp; ch 3, sk last ch-3 sp, sc in next dc and in 2nd ch of turning ch-2. Ch 1, turn.

Row 7:
Sc in first 2 sc and in next ch-3 sp, ch 3, sk next sc, sc in next sc, ch 3; * sc in next ch-3 sp, in next sc, and in next ch-3 sp; ch 3, sk next sc, sc in next sc, ch 3; rep from * to last ch-3 sp; sc in last ch-3 sp and in last 2 sc. Ch 1, turn.

Row 8:
Sc in first 3 sc and in next ch-3 sp, ch 5; * sc in next ch-3 sp, in next 3 sc, and in next ch-3 sp; ch 5; rep from * to last ch-3 sp; sc in last ch-3 sp and in last 3 sc. Ch 1, turn.

Rep Rows 3 through 8 for desired length.

Last Row:
Sc in each sc and in 3rd ch of each ch-5 sp.

Finish off.

#12

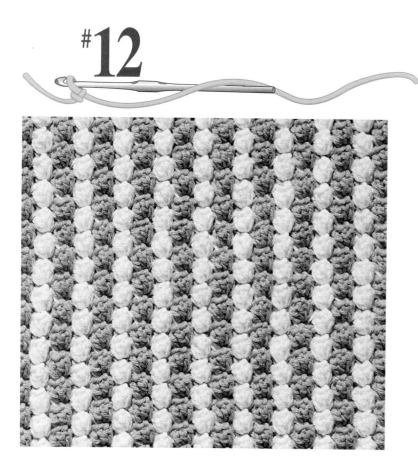

Materials:
Yarn—Color A (light); Color B (dark)

Pattern Stitch

Popcorn (PC):
5 dc in st indicated; drop lp from hook, insert hook in first dc made, draw dropped lp through— PC made.

Instructions
Foundation ch with Color A: multiple of 8 + 2

Row 1 (wrong side):
Sc in 2nd ch from hook and in each rem ch. Ch 1, turn.

Row 2 (right side):
Sc in first 2 sc, ch 2, sk next sc, PC (see Pattern Stitch) in next sc; * ch 2, sk next sc, sc in next sc, ch 2, sk next sc, PC in next sc; rep from * to last sc; dc in last sc. Finish off Color A. Do not turn.

Row 3:
Hold piece with right side facing you; join Color B in first sc of prev row; ch 3, PC in next sc; ch 2; * sc in top of next PC, ch 2, PC in next sc; ch 2; rep from * to last PC; sc in top of last PC and in last dc. Finish off Color B. Do not turn.

Row 4:
Hold piece with right side facing you; join Color A in 3rd ch of beg ch-3 of prev row; ch 1, sc in same ch as joining and in top of next PC, ch 2, PC in next sc; * ch 2, sc in top of next PC, ch 2, PC in next sc; rep from * to last sc; dc in last sc. Finish off Color A. Do not turn.

Rep Rows 3 and 4 for desired length. At end of last row, do not finish off Color A. Ch 1, turn.

Last Row:
Sc in each st and in each ch-2 sp.

Finish off.

#13

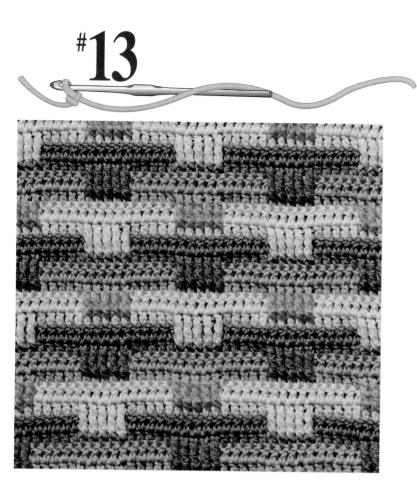

Materials:
Yarn—Color A **(dark)**; Color B **(off white)**;
    Color C **(light)**

Color Sequence:
2 rows Color A
2 rows Color B
2 rows Color C

Pattern Stitch

Front Post Double Triple Crochet (FPdtrc):
YO 3 times, insert hook from front to back to front around post **(see page 7)** of next dc on 2nd row below, draw up lp, **(**YO, draw through 2 lps on hook**)** 4 times—FPdtrc made. **Note:** Sk dc behind FPdtrc.

Instructions
Foundation ch with Color A: multiple of 20 + 16

Row 1 (right side):
Dc in 3rd ch from hook **(2 skipped chs count as a dc)** and in each rem ch. Ch 2 **(counts as first dc on following rows)**, turn.

Row 2:
Dc in each dc to beg 2 skipped chs; dc in 2nd ch of beg 2 skipped chs. Change to next color in sequence by drawing lp through; cut prev color. Ch 2, turn.

Row 3:
Dc in next 4 dc; **✱** FPdtrc (see Pattern Stitch) around each of next 5 dc on 2nd row below; on working row, dc in next 15 dc; rep from **✱** to last 10 sts; FPdtrc around each of next 5 dc on 2nd row below; dc in last 4 dc and in 2nd ch of turning ch-2. Ch 2, turn.

Row 4:
Dc in each st to turning ch-2; dc in 2nd ch of turning ch-2. Change to next color in sequence by drawing lp through; cut prev color. Ch 2, turn.

Row 5:
Dc in next 14 dc; **✱** FPdtrc around each of next 5 dc on 2nd row below; on working row, dc in next 15 dc; rep from **✱** across, working last dc in 2nd ch of turning ch-2. Ch 2, turn.

Row 6:
Rep Row 4.

Working in color sequence, rep Rows 3 through 6 for desired length. At end of last row, do not ch 2; do not turn.

Finish off.

#14

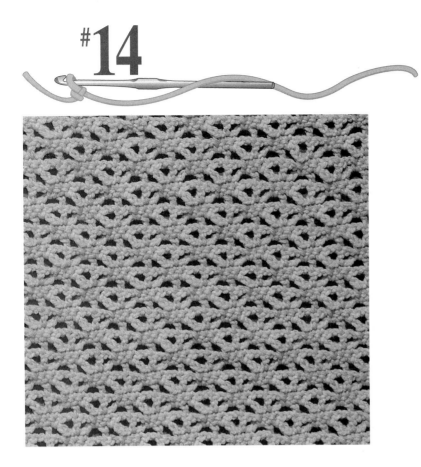

Materials:
Yarn—One color

Instructions
Foundation ch: multiple of 8 + 4

Row 1 (right side):
Sc in 7th ch from hook **(6 skipped chs count as a ch-2 sp, a dc, and a ch-2 sp)** and in next 2 chs; ***** ch 2, sk next 2 chs, dc in next ch, ch 2, sk next 2 chs, sc in next 3 chs; rep from ***** to last 3 chs; ch 2, sk next 2 chs, dc in next ch. Ch 1, turn.

Row 2:
Sc in first dc and in next ch-2 sp, ch 2, sk next sc, dc in next sc, ch 2; ***** sc in next ch-2 sp, in next dc, and in next ch-2 sp; ch 2, sk next sc, dc in next sc, ch 2; rep from ***** to beg 6 skipped chs; sk next ch of beg 6 skipped chs, sc in next 2 chs. Ch 1, turn.

Row 3:
Sc in first 2 sc, ch 2, dc in next dc, ch 2; ***** sc in next 3 sc, ch 2, dc in next dc, ch 2; rep from ***** to last 2 sc; sc in last 2 sc. Ch 4 **(counts as first dc and ch-2 sp on following rows)**, turn.

Row 4:
Sc in next ch-2 sp, in next dc, and in next ch-2 sp; ***** ch 2, sk next sc, dc in next sc, ch 2, sc in next ch-2 sp, in next dc, and in next ch-2 sp; rep from ***** to last 2 sc; ch 2, sk next sc, dc in last sc. Ch 4, turn.

Row 5:
Sc in next 3 sc; ***** ch 2, dc in next dc, ch 2, sc in next 3 sc; rep from ***** to turning ch-4; ch 2, sk next 2 chs of turning ch, dc in next ch. Ch 1, turn.

Row 6:
Sc in first dc and in next ch-2 sp, ch 2, sk next sc, dc in next sc, ch 2; ***** sc in next ch-2 sp, in next dc, and in next ch-2 sp; ch 2, sk next sc, dc in next sc, ch 2; rep from ***** to turning ch-4; sk next ch of turning ch, sc in next 2 chs. Ch 1, turn.

Rep Rows 3 through 6 for desired length, ending with Row 4. At end of last row, do not ch 4; do not turn.

Finish off.

#15

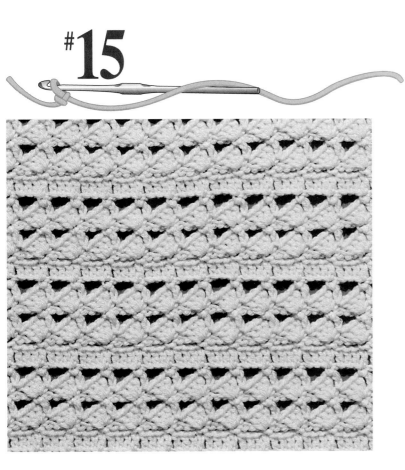

Materials:
Yarn—One color

Instructions
Foundation ch: multiple of 4 + 2

Row 1 (right side):
Dc in 3rd ch from hook (2 skipped chs count as a dc) and in each rem ch. Ch 1, turn.

Row 2:
Sc in first dc, ch 3, sk next 3 dc; * sc in next dc, ch 3, sk next 3 dc; rep from * to beg 2 skipped chs; sc in 2nd ch of beg 2 skipped chs. Ch 2 (counts as first dc on following rows), turn.

Row 3:
3 dc in first sc; * in next sc work (sc, ch 3, 3 dc); rep from * to last sc; sc in last sc. Ch 5 (counts as first dc and ch-3 sp on following rows), turn.

Row 4:
* Sc in next ch-3 sp, ch 3; rep from * to turning ch-2; sc in sp formed by turning ch-2. Ch 2, turn.

Row 5:
3 dc in first sc; * in next sc work (sc, ch 3, 3 dc); rep from * to turning ch-5; sk next 3 chs of turning ch, sc in next ch. Ch 5, turn.

Row 6:
Rep Row 4.

Row 7:
Dc in each ch and in each sc to turning ch-5; dc in next 4 chs of turning ch-5. Ch 1, turn.

Row 8:
Sc in first dc, ch 3, sk next 3 dc; * sc in next dc, ch 3, sk next 3 dc; rep from * to turning ch-2; sc in 2nd ch of turning ch-2. Ch 2, turn.

Rep Rows 3 through 8 for desired length, ending with Row 7. At end of last row, do not ch 1; do not turn.

Finish off.

#16

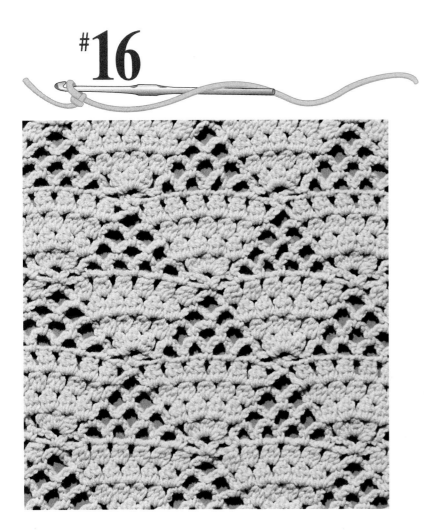

Materials:
Yarn—One color

Pattern Stitch

Cluster (CL):
Keeping last lp of each dc on hook, 3 dc in st indicated; YO and draw through all 4 lps on hook—CL made.

Instructions
Foundation ch: multiple of 20 + 4

Row 1 (right side):
Sc in 6th ch from hook (5 skipped chs count as a ch-1 sp, a dc, and a ch-2 sp), ch 5, sk next 3 chs, sc in next ch, ch 1, sk next 3 chs, in next ch work [CL (see Pattern Stitch), ch 1] 3 times; * sk next 3 chs, sc in next ch, (ch 5, sk next 3 chs, sc in next ch) 3 times; ch 1, sk next 3 chs, in next ch work (CL, ch 1) 3 times; rep from * to last 10 chs; sk next 3 chs, sc in next ch, ch 5, sk next 3 chs, sc in next ch, ch 2, sk next ch, dc in next ch. Ch 1, turn.

Row 2:
Sc in first dc, ch 5, sk next ch-2 sp, sc in next ch-5 sp, ch 1, sk next sc, (CL in next ch-1 sp, ch 1) 4 times; * sc in next ch-5 sp, (ch 5, sc in next ch-5 sp) twice; ch 1, sk next sc, (CL in next ch-1 sp, ch 1) 4 times; rep from * to last ch-5 sp; sc in last ch-5 sp, ch 5, sk next 2 chs of beg 5 skipped chs, sc in next ch. Ch 4 (counts as first dc and ch-2 sp on following rows), turn.

Row 3:
Sc in next ch-5 sp, ch 1, sk next sc, (CL in next ch-1 sp, ch 1) 5 times; * sc in next ch-5 sp, ch 5, sc in next ch-5 sp, ch 1, sk next sc, (CL in next ch-1 sp, ch 1) 5 times; rep from * to last ch-5 sp; sc in last ch-5 sp, ch 2, dc in last sc. Ch 1, turn.

Row 4:
Sc in first dc, ch 2, sk next sc, (CL in next ch-1 sp, ch 2) 6 times; * sc in next ch-5 sp, ch 2, sk next sc, (CL in next ch-1 sp, ch 2) 6 times; rep from * to turning ch-4; sk next 2 chs of turning ch, sc in next ch. Ch 4, turn.

Row 5:
Sk next ch-2 sp, sc in next ch-2 sp, (ch 5, sc in next ch-2 sp) 4 times; * ch 1, sk next ch-2 sp, in next

sc work (dc, ch 1) twice; sk next ch-2 sp, sc in next ch-2 sp, (ch 5, sc in next ch-2 sp) 4 times; rep from * to last ch-2 sp; ch 2, sk last ch-2 sp, dc in last sc. Ch 2 (counts as first dc on following rows), turn.

Row 6:
In first dc work (dc, ch 1, CL); ch 1, sk next ch-2 sp, sc in next ch-5 sp, (ch 5, sc in next ch-5 sp) 3 times; * ch 1, sk next ch-1 sp, in next ch-1 sp work (CL, ch 1) 3 times; sk next ch-1 sp, sc in next ch-5 sp, (ch 5, sc in next ch-5 sp) 3 times; rep from * to turning ch-4; ch 1, sk next 2 chs of turning ch, in next ch work (CL, ch 1, 2 dc). Ch 2, turn.

Row 7:
(CL in next ch-1 sp, ch 1) twice; sc in next ch-5 sp, (ch 5, sc in next ch-5 sp) twice; * ch 1, sk next sc, (CL in next ch-1 sp, ch 1) 4 times; sc in next ch-5 sp, (ch 5, sc in next ch-5 sp) twice; rep from * to last sc; sk last sc, (ch 1, CL in next ch-1 sp) twice; dc in 2nd ch of turning ch-2. Ch 2, turn.

Row 8:
Dc in first dc, ch 1, (CL in next ch-1 sp, ch 1) twice; sc in next ch-5 sp, ch 5, sc in next ch-5 sp; * ch 1, sk next sc, (CL in next ch-1 sp, ch 1) 5 times; sc in next ch-5 sp, ch 5, sc in next ch-5 sp; rep from * to last 2 CLs; ch 1, (CL in next ch-1 sp, ch 1) twice; 2 dc in 2nd ch of turning ch-2. Ch 3 (counts as first dc and ch-1 sp on following rows), turn.

Row 9:
(CL in next ch-1 sp, ch 2) 3 times; sc in next ch-5 sp; * ch 2, (CL in next ch-1 sp, ch 2) 6 times; sc in next ch-5 sp; rep from * to last 2 CLs; (ch 2, CL in next ch-1 sp) 3 times; ch 1, dc in 2nd ch of turning ch-2. Ch 1, turn.

Row 10:
Sc in first dc, ch 5, sk next ch-1 sp, sc in next ch-2 sp, ch 5, sc in next ch-2 sp, ch 1, sk next ch-2 sp, in next sc work (dc, ch 1) twice; * sk next ch-2 sp, sc in next ch-2 sp, (ch 5, sc in next ch-2 sp) 4 times; ch 1, sk next ch-2 sp, in next sc work (dc, ch 1) twice; rep from * to last 3 CLs; sk next ch-2 sp, (sc in next ch-2 sp, ch 5) twice; sk next CL and next ch of turning ch-3, sc in next ch. Ch 4, turn.

Row 11:
Sc in next ch-5 sp, ch 5, sc in next ch-5 sp, ch 1, sk next ch-1 sp, in next ch-1 sp work (CL, ch 1) 3 times; * sk next ch-1 sp, sc in next ch-5 sp, (ch 5, sc in next ch-5 sp) 3 times; ch 1, sk next ch-1 sp, in next ch-1 sp work (CL, ch 1) 3 times; rep from * to last 2 ch-5 sps; sc in next ch-5 sp, ch 5, sc in next ch-5 sp, ch 2, dc in next sc. Ch 1, turn.

Row 12:
Sc in first dc, ch 5, sk next ch-2 sp, sc in next ch-5 sp, ch 1, sk next sc, (CL in next ch-1 sp, ch 1) 4 times; * sc in next ch-5 sp, (ch 5, sc in next ch-5 sp) twice; ch 1, sk next sc, (CL in next ch-1 sp, ch 1) 4 times; rep from * to last ch-5 sp; sc in last ch-5 sp, ch 5, sk next 2 chs of turning ch-4, sc in next ch. Ch 4, turn.

Rep Rows 3 through 12 for desired length, ending with Row 4. At end of last row, do not ch 4; do not turn.

Finish off.

#17

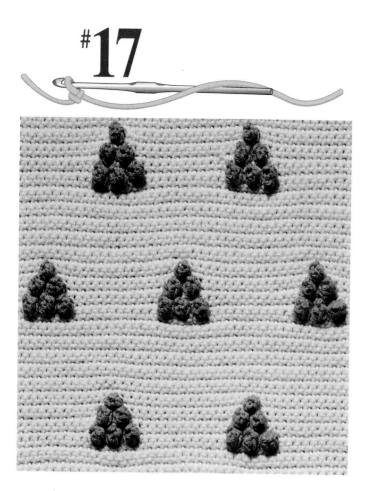

Materials:
Yarn—Color A (light); Color B (dark)

Pattern Stitch

Popcorn (PC):
4 dc in st indicated; drop lp from hook, insert hook in first dc made, draw dropped lp through; ch 1—PC made.

Instructions
Foundation ch with Color A: multiple of 16 + 2

Row 1 (wrong side):
Sc in 2nd ch from hook and in each rem ch. Ch 1, turn.

Row 2 (right side):
Sc in each sc. Ch 1, turn.

Rows 3 through 7:
Rep Row 2.

Note: On following rows, change colors by drawing lp of new color through last lp of old color.

Row 8:
Sc in first 2 sc; change to Color B; cut Color A; PC (see Pattern Stitch) in next sc; (sc in next sc, PC in next sc) twice; * change to Color A; cut Color B; sc in next 11 sc; change to Color B; cut Color A; PC in next sc; (sc in next sc, PC in next sc) twice; rep from * to last 10 sc; sc in last 10 sc. Ch 1, turn.

Row 9:
Sc in each sc and in ch-1 sp at top of each PC. Ch 1, turn.

Row 10:
Sc in first 3 sc; change to Color B; cut Color A; PC in next sc; sc in next sc, PC in next sc; * change to Color A; cut Color B; sc in next 13 sc; change to Color B; cut Color A; PC in next sc; sc in next sc, PC in next sc; rep from * to last 11 sc; sc in last 11 sc. Ch 1, turn.

Row 11:
Rep Row 9.

Row 12:
Sc in first 4 sc; change to Color B; drop Color A; PC in next sc; change to Color A; cut Color B; * sc in next 15 sc; change to Color B; drop Color A; PC in next sc; change to Color A; cut Color B; rep from * to last 12 sc; sc in last 12 sc. Ch 1, turn.

Row 13:
Rep Row 9.

Rows 14 through 25:
Rep Row 2.

Row 26:
Sc in first 10 sc; change to Color B; cut Color A; PC in next sc; (sc in next sc, PC in next sc) twice; * change to Color A; cut Color B; sc in next 11 sc; change to Color B; cut Color A; PC in next sc; (sc in next sc, PC in next sc) twice; rep from * to last 2 sc; sc in last 2 sc. Ch 1, turn.

Row 27:
Rep Row 9.

continued

Row 28:
Sc in first 11 sc; change to Color B; cut Color A; PC in next sc, sc in next sc, PC in next sc; * change to Color A; cut Color B; sc in next 13 sc; change to Color B; cut Color A; PC in next sc; sc in next sc, PC in next sc; rep from * to last 3 sc; sc in last 3 sc. Ch 1, turn.

Row 29:
Rep Row 9.

Row 30:
Sc in first 12 sc; change to Color B; drop Color A; PC in next sc; change to Color A; cut Color B; * sc in next 15 sc; change to Color B; drop Color A; PC in next sc; change to Color A; cut Color B; rep from * to last 4 sc; sc in last 4 sc. Ch 1, turn.

Row 31:
Rep Row 9.

Rows 32 through 37:
Rep Row 2.

Rep Rows 2 through 37 for desired length. At end of last row, do not ch 1; do not turn.

Finish off.

#18

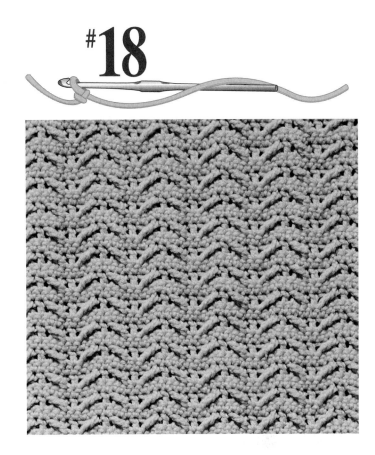

Materials:
Yarn—One color

Pattern Stitches

Cross Right (CrR):
Sk next 2 sc, trc in next sc, working behind trc just worked, dc in 2 skipped sc—CrR made.

Cross Left (CrL):
Sk next sc, dc in next 2 sc, working in front of dc just made, trc in skipped sc—CrL made.

Instructions
Foundation ch: multiple of 8 + 2

Row 1 (wrong side):
Sc in 2nd ch from hook and in each rem ch.
Ch 2 (counts as first dc on following rows), turn.

Row 2 (right side):
* CrR (see Pattern Stitches); dc in next sc, CrL (see Pattern Stitches); dc in next sc; rep from * across. Ch 1, turn.

Row 3:
Sc in each st to turning ch-2; sc in 2nd ch of turning ch-2. Ch 2, turn.

Rep Rows 2 and 3 for desired length. At end of last row, do not ch 2; do not turn.

Finish off.

#19

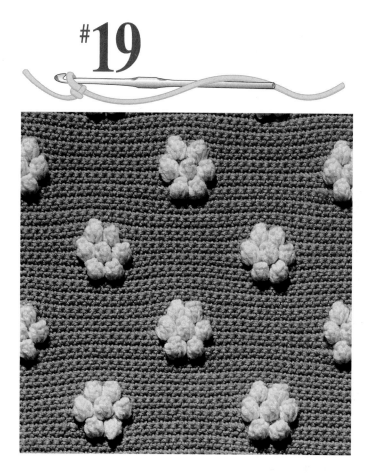

Materials:

Yarn—Color A (dark); Color B (off white);
  Color C (light)

Pattern Stitch

Popcorn (PC):
5 dc in st indicated; drop lp from hook, insert hook
in first dc made, draw dropped lp through; ch 1—
PC made.

Instructions

Foundation ch with Color A: multiple of 20 + 2

Row 1 (wrong side):
Sc in 2nd ch from hook and in each rem ch. Ch 1, turn.

Row 2 (right side):
Sc in each sc. Ch 1, turn.

Rows 3 through 7:
Rep Row 2.

Note: On following rows, change colors by drawing lp
of new color through last lp of old color.

Row 8:
Sc in first 4 sc; change to Color B; cut Color A; PC (see
Pattern Stitch) in next sc; sc in next sc, PC in next sc;
change to Color A; cut Color B; * sc in next 17 sc;
change to Color B; cut Color A; PC in next sc; sc in

next sc, PC in next sc; change to Color A; cut Color B;
rep from * to last 14 sc; sc in last 14 sc. Ch 1, turn.

Row 9:
Sc in each sc and in ch-1 sp at top of each PC.
Ch 1, turn.

Row 10:
Sc in first 3 sc; *† change to Color B; cut Color A;
PC in next sc; sc in next sc; change to Color C; drop
Color B; PC in next sc; change to Color B; cut Color C;
sc in next sc, PC in next sc; change to Color A; cut
Color B †; sc in next 15 sc; rep from * to last 18 sc;
rep from † to † once; sc in last 13 sc. Ch 1, turn.

Row 11:
Rep Row 9.

Rows 12 and 13:
Rep Rows 8 and 9.

Rows 14 through 19:
Rep Row 2.

Row 20:
Sc in first 14 sc; change to Color B; cut Color A; PC in
next sc; sc in next sc, PC in next sc; change to Color A;
cut Color B; * sc in next 17 sc; change to Color B; cut
Color A; PC in next sc; sc in next sc, PC in next sc;
change to Color A; cut Color B; rep from * across to
last 4 sc; sc in last 4 sc. Ch 1, turn.

Row 21:
Rep Row 9.

Row 22:
Sc in first 13 sc; *† change to Color B; cut Color A;
PC in next sc; sc in next sc; change to Color C; drop
Color B; PC in next sc; change to Color B; cut Color C;
sc in next sc, PC in next sc; change to Color A; cut
Color B †; sc in next 15 sc; rep from * to last 8 sc; rep
from † to † once; sc in last 3 sc. Ch 1, turn.

Row 23:
Rep Row 9.

Row 24:
Rep Row 20.

Row 25:
Rep Row 9.

Rep Rows 2 through 25 for desired length, ending with
Row 7. At end of last row, do not ch 1; do not turn.

Finish off.

#20

Materials:

Yarn—Color A (dark); Color B (light)

Pattern Stitch

Puff Stitch (puff st):

(YO, insert hook in same st, draw up lp) 3 times; YO, draw through 6 lps on hook; YO and draw through 2 lps on hook—puff st made. Push to right side.

Instructions

Foundation ch with Color A: multiple of 2

Row 1 (wrong side):

Dc in 3rd ch from hook, (beg 2 skipped chs count as a dc) and in each rem ch. Ch 2 (counts as first dc on following rows), turn.

Row 2 (right side):

Dc in each dc to beg 2 skipped chs; dc in 2nd ch of beg 2 skipped chs; change to Color B by drawing lp through; cut Color A. Ch 1, turn.

Row 3:

In first dc work [sc, puff st (see Pattern Stitch)]; * sk next dc, in next dc work (sc, puff st); rep from * to last 2 sts; sk next dc, sc in 2nd ch of turning ch-2. Ch 1, turn.

Row 4:

In first sc work (sc, puff st); * sk next puff st, in next sc work (sc, puff st); rep from * to last 2 sts; sk last puff st, sc in last sc; change to Color A by drawing lp through; cut Color B. Ch 2, turn.

Row 5:

Dc in each puff st and in each sc. Ch 2, turn.

Row 6:

Dc in each dc to turning ch-2; dc in 2nd ch of turning ch-2; change to Color B by drawing lp through; cut Color A. Ch 1, turn.

Rep Rows 3 through 6 for desired length. At end of last row, do not ch 1; do not turn.

Finish off.

#21

Materials:
Yarn—One color

Pattern Stitches

Front Post Double Crochet (FPdc):
YO, insert hook from front to back to front around post (see page 7) of next dc, draw up lp, (YO, draw through 2 lps on hook) twice—FPdc made.

Back Post Double Crochet (BPdc):
YO, insert hook from back to front to back around post (see page 7) of next dc, draw up lp, (YO, draw through 2 lps on hook) twice—BPdc made.

Instructions
Foundation ch: multiple of 6 + 3

Row 1 (right side):
Dc in 3rd ch from hook (2 skipped chs count as a dc) and in each rem ch. Ch 2 (counts as first dc on following rows), turn.

Row 2:
* FPdc (see Pattern Stitches) around each of next 3 dc; BPdc (see Pattern Stitches) around each of next 3 dc; rep from * to beg 2 skipped chs; dc in 2nd ch of beg 2 skipped chs. Ch 2, turn.

Row 3:
* FPdc around each of next 3 BPdc; BPdc around each of next 3 FPdc; rep from * to turning ch-2; dc in 2nd ch of turning ch-2. Ch 2, turn.

Row 4:
* BPdc around each of next 3 BPdc; FPdc around each of next 3 FPdc; rep from * to turning ch-2; dc in 2nd ch of turning ch-2. Ch 2, turn.

Row 5:
* BPdc around each of next 3 FPdc; FPdc around each of next 3 BPdc; rep from * to turning ch-2; dc in 2nd ch of turning ch-2. Ch 2, turn.

Row 6:
* FPdc around each of next 3 FPdc; BPdc around each of next 3 BPdc; rep from * to turning ch-2; dc in 2nd ch of turning ch-2. Ch 2, turn.

Rep Rows 3 through 6 for desired length, ending with Row 3. At end of last row, do not ch 2; do not turn.

Finish off.

#22

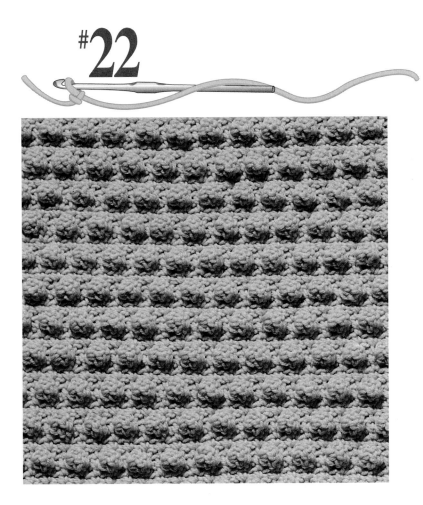

Materials:

Yarn—One color

Instructions

Foundation ch: multiple of 4 + 2

Row 1 (right side):
Sc in 2nd ch from hook; * ch 1, sk next ch, sc in next ch; rep from * across. Ch 1, turn.

Row 2:
Sc in first sc; * ch 4, 2 dc in 4th ch from hook—puff st made; sc in next sc, ch 1, sc in next sc; rep from * across. Ch 1, turn.

Row 3:
Sc in first sc; * ch 1, sc in next sc, ch 1, working behind puff st, sc in next sc; rep from * across. Ch 1, turn.

Row 4:
Sc in first sc; * ch 1, sc in next sc; rep from * across. Ch 1, turn.

Row 5:
Rep Row 4.

Row 6:
Sc in first sc; * ch 1, sc in next sc, puff st; sc in next sc; rep from * across. Ch 1, turn.

Row 7:
Sc in first sc; * ch 1, working behind puff st, sc in next sc, ch 1, sc in next sc; rep from * across. Ch 1, turn.

Rows 8 and 9:
Rep Row 4.

Rep Rows 2 through 9 for desired length, ending with Row 5. At end of last row, do not ch 1; do not turn.

Finish off.

#23

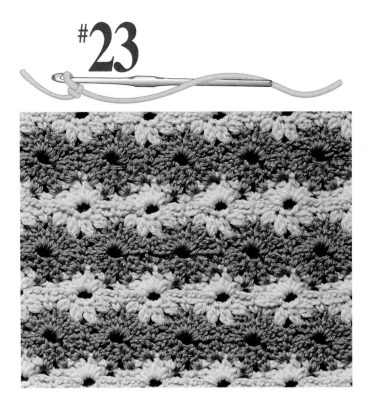

Materials:
Yarn—Color A (dark); Color B (light)

Pattern Stitch

Cluster (CL):
Keeping last lp of each dc on hook, 2 dc in st indicated; YO and draw through all 3 lps on hook—CL made.

Instructions
Foundation ch with Color A: multiple of 11 + 3

Row 1 (right side):
Sc in 2nd ch from hook, ch 1, sk next ch, sc in next ch, (ch 3, sk next 3 chs, sc in next ch) twice; * ch 2, sk next 2 chs, sc in next ch, (ch 3, sk next 3 chs, sc in next ch) twice; rep from * to last 2 chs; ch 1, sk next ch, sc in last ch. Ch 2, turn.

Row 2:
In next ch-1 sp work [CL (see Pattern Stitch), ch 2, CL]; ch 1, sk next ch-3 sp, sc in next sc; * ch 1, sk next ch-3 sp, in next ch-2 sp work (CL, ch 2) 3 times; CL in same sp; ch 1, sk next ch-3 sp, sc in next sc; rep from * to last ch-3 sp; ch 1, sk last ch-3 sp, in next ch-1 sp work (CL, ch 2, CL); dc in next sc; change to Color B by drawing lp through; cut Color A. Ch 1, turn.

Row 3:
Sc in first dc; * ch 3, CL in top each of next 4 CLs; ch 3, sc in next ch-2 sp; rep from * across, working last sc in 2nd ch of turning ch-2. Ch 1, turn.

Row 4:
Sc in first sc; * ch 3, sc in top of next CL, ch 2, sk next 2 CLs, sc in top of next CL, ch 3, sc in next sc; rep from * across. Ch 1, turn.

Row 5:
Sc in first sc; * ch 1, sk next ch-3 sp, in next ch-2 sp work (CL, ch 2) 3 times; CL in same sp; ch 1, sk next ch-3 sp, sc in next sc; rep from * across; change to Color A by drawing lp through; cut Color B. Ch 2, turn.

Row 6:
CL in top of each of next 2 CLs; ch 3, sc in next ch-2 sp, ch 3; * CL in top of each of next 4 CLs; ch 3, sc in next ch-2 sp, ch 3; rep from * to last 2 CLs; CL in top of each of last 2 CLs; dc in last sc. Ch 1, turn.

Row 7:
Sc in first dc, ch 1, sk next CL, sc in next CL, ch 3, sc in next sc, ch 3; * sc in top of next CL, ch 2, sk next 2 CLs, sc in top of next CL, ch 3, sc in next sc, ch 3; rep from * to last 2 CLs; sc in next CL, ch 1, sk last CL, sc in 2nd ch of turning ch-2. Ch 2, turn.

Row 8:
In next ch-1 sp work (CL, ch 2, CL); ch 1, sk next ch-3 sp, sc in next sc; * ch 1, sk next ch-3 sp, in next ch-2 sp work (CL, ch 2) 3 times; CL in same sp; ch 1, sk next ch-3 sp, sc in next sc; rep from * to last ch-3 sp; ch 1, sk last ch-3 sp, in next ch-1 sp work (CL, ch 2, CL); dc in next sc; change to Color B by drawing lp through; cut Color A. Ch 1, turn.

Rep Rows 3 through 8 for desired length, ending with Row 7. At end of last row, do not ch 2; do not turn.

Finish off.

#24

Materials:
Yarn—One color

Pattern Stitches

Front Post Double Crochet (FPdc):
YO, insert hook from front to back to front around post (see page 7) of next dc, draw up lp, (YO, draw through 2 lps on hook) twice—FPdc made.
Note: Sk dc behind FPdc.

Back Post Double Crochet (BPdc):
YO, insert hook from back to front to back around post (see page 7) of next dc, draw up lp, (YO, draw through 2 lps on hook) twice—BPdc made.
Note: Sk dc behind BPdc.

Instructions
Foundation ch: multiple of 8 + 3

Row 1 (right side):
Dc in 3rd ch from hook (2 skipped chs count as a dc) and in each rem ch. Ch 2 (counts as first dc on following rows), turn.

Row 2:
* FPdc (see Pattern Stitches) around each of next 4 dc; BPdc (see Pattern Stitches) around each of next 4 dc; rep from * to beg 2 skipped chs; dc in 2nd ch of beg 2 skipped chs. Ch 2, turn.

Row 3:
BPdc around next st; FPdc around each of next 4 sts; * BPdc around each of next 4 sts; FPdc around each of next 4 sts; rep from * to last 4 sts; BPdc around each of next 3 sts; dc in 2nd ch of turning ch-2. Ch 2, turn.

Row 4:
FPdc around each of next 2 sts; BPdc around each of next 4 sts; * FPdc around each of next 4 sts; BPdc around each of next 4 sts; rep from * to last 3 sts; FPdc around each of next 2 sts; dc in 2nd ch of turning ch-2. Ch 2, turn.

Row 5:
BPdc around each of next 3 sts; FPdc around each of next 4 sts; * BPdc around each of next 4 sts; FPdc around each of next 4 sts; rep from * to last 2 sts; BPdc around next st; dc in 2nd ch of turning ch-2. Ch 2, turn.

Row 6:
* BPdc around each of next 4 sts; FPdc around each of next 4 sts; rep from * to turning ch-2; dc in 2nd ch of turning ch-2. Ch 2, turn.

Row 7:
FPdc around next st; BPdc around each of next 4 sts; * FPdc around each of next 4 sts; BPdc around each of next 4 sts; rep from * to last 4 sts; FPdc around each of next 3 sts; dc in 2nd ch of turning ch-2. Ch 2, turn.

Row 8:
BPdc around each of next 2 sts; FPdc around each of next 4 sts; * BPdc around each of next 4 sts; FPdc around each of next 4 sts; rep from * to last 3 sts; BPdc around each of next 2 sts; dc in 2nd ch of turning ch-2. Ch 2, turn.

Row 9:
FPdc around each of next 3 sts; BPdc around each of next 4 sts; * FPdc around each of next 4 sts; BPdc around each of next 4 sts; rep from * to last 2 sts; FPdc around next st; dc in 2nd ch of turning ch-2. Ch 2, turn.

Row 10:
* FPdc around each of next 4 sts; BPdc around each of next 4 sts; rep from * to turning ch-2; dc in 2nd ch of turning ch-2. Ch 2, turn.

Rep Rows 3 through 10 for desired length. At end of last row, do not ch 2; do not turn.

Finish off.

#25

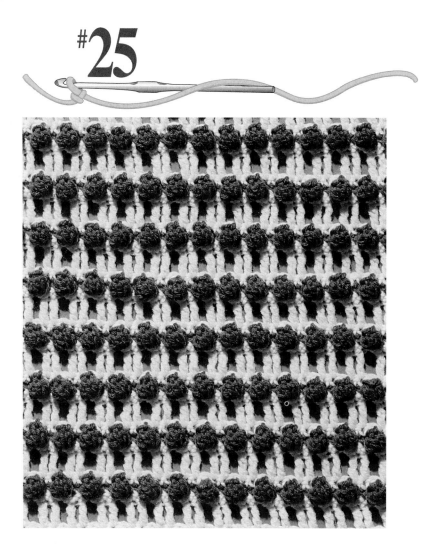

Materials:
Yarn—Color A (light); Color B (dark)

Pattern Stitch

Popcorn (PC):
5 dc in st indicated; drop lp from hook, insert hook in first dc made, draw dropped lp through; ch 1, pull tight—PC made.

Instructions
Foundation ch with Color A: multiple of 3

Row 1 (wrong side):
Sc in 2nd ch from hook and in each rem ch; change to Color B by drawing lp through; cut Color A. Ch 1, turn.

Row 2 (right side):
Sc in first 2 sc; * PC (see Pattern Stitch) in next sc; sc in next 2 sc; rep from * across; change to Color A by drawing lp through; cut Color B. Ch 1, turn.

Row 3:
Sc in first 2 sc; * ch 1, sk next PC, sc in next 2 sc; rep from * across. Ch 3 (counts as first trc on following rows), turn.

Row 4:
Trc in next sc; * ch 1, sk next ch-1 sp, trc in next 2 sc; rep from * across. Ch 1, turn.

Row 5:
Sc in each trc and in each ch to last 2 sts; sc in last trc and in 3rd ch of turning ch-3; change to Color B by drawing lp through; cut Color A. Ch 1, turn.

Rep Rows 2 through 5 for desired length.

Next Row:
Rep Row 2.

Last Row:
Sc in each sc and in top of each PC.

Finish off.

17

18

19

20

21

22

23

24

25

26

27

28

29

30

31

32

33

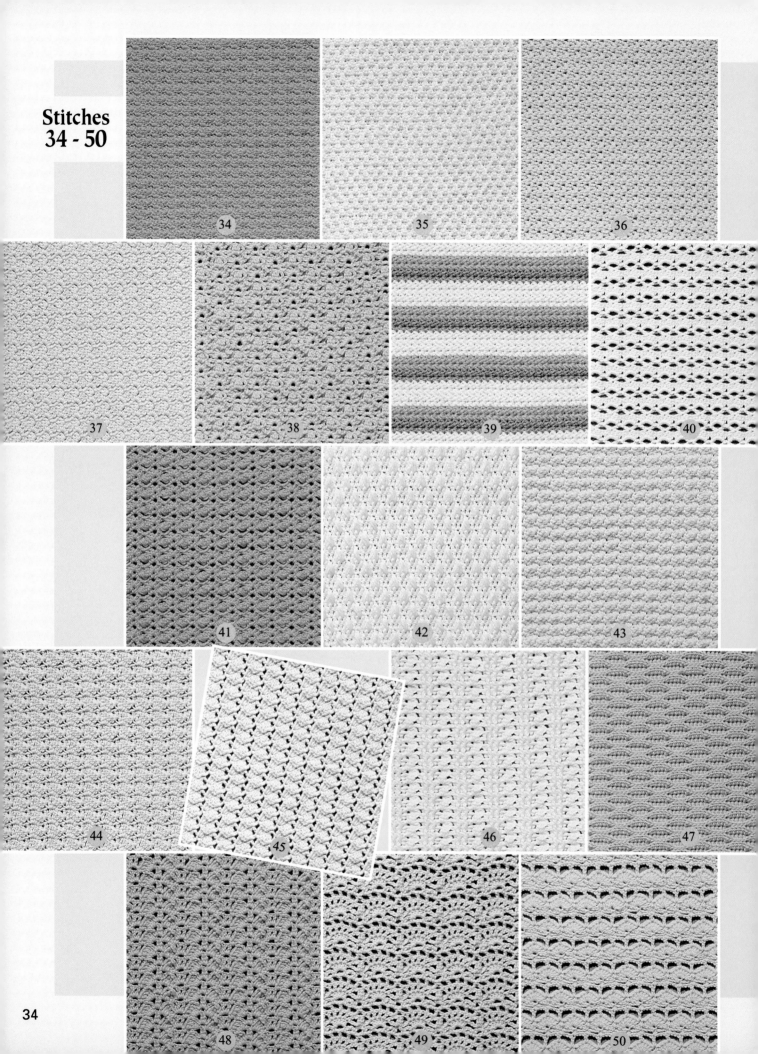

Stitches 34 - 50

34

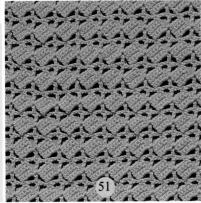

51

52

53

Stitches 51 - 67

54

55

56

57

58

59

60

61

62

63

64

65

66

67

35

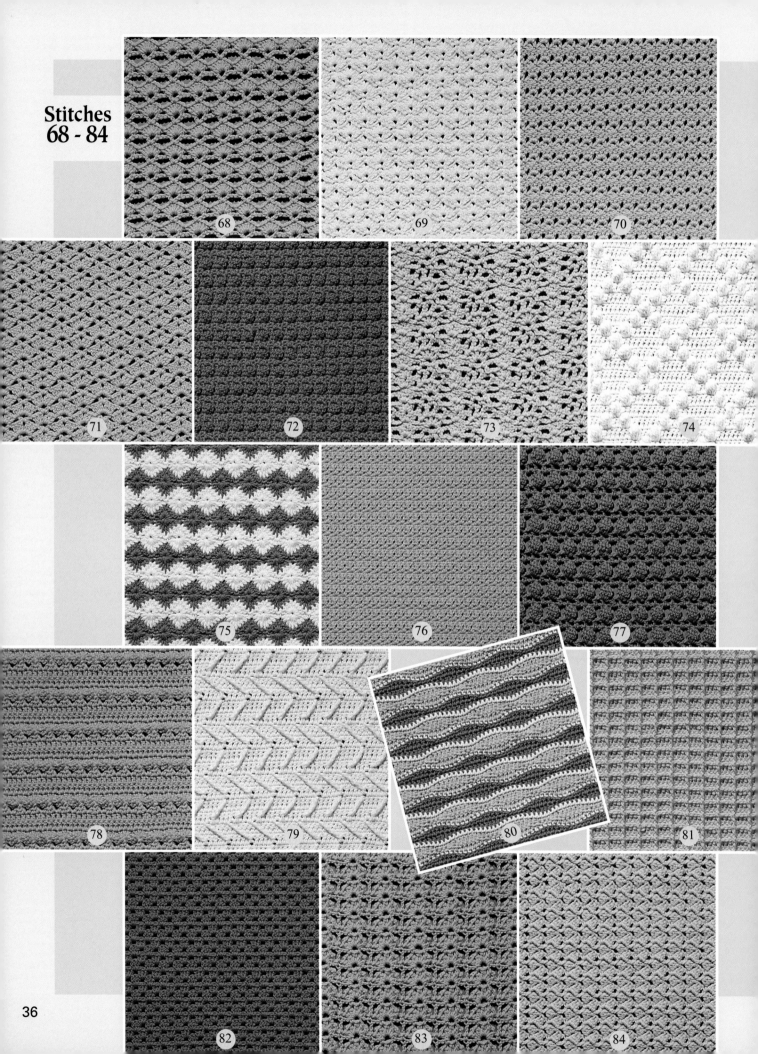

Stitches
68 - 84

68

69

70

71

72

73

74

75

76

77

78

79

80

81

82

83

84

36

#26

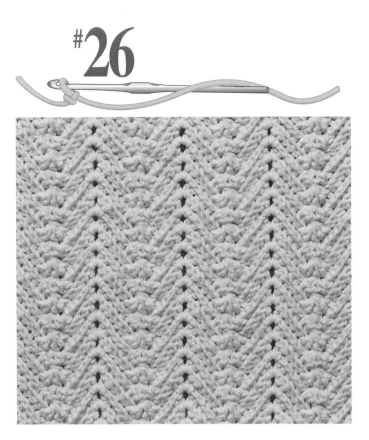

Materials:
Yarn—One color

Pattern Stitches

Back Post Double Crochet (BPdc):
YO, insert hook from back to front to back around post (see page 7) of next st, draw up lp, (YO, draw through 2 lps on hook) twice—BPdc made.

Front Post Double Crochet (FPdc):
YO, insert hook from front to back to front around post (see page 7) of next st, draw up lp, (YO, draw through 2 lps on hook) twice—FPdc made.

2-Back Post Double Crochet Cluster (2-BPdc CL):
Keeping last lp of each st on hook, BPdc around each of next 2 sts; YO and draw through all 3 lps on hook—2-BPdc CL made.

2-Front Post Double Crochet Cluster (2-FPdc CL):
Keeping last lp of each st on hook, FPdc around each of next 2 dc; YO and draw through all 3 lps on hook—2-FPdc CL made.

continued in next column

3-Back Post Double Crochet Cluster (3-BPdc CL):
Keeping last lp of each st on hook, BPdc around each of next 2 dc and around next cluster; YO and draw through all 4 lps on hook—3-BPdc CL made.

3-Front Post Double Crochet Cluster (3-FPdc CL):
Keeping last lp of each st on hook, FPdc around each of next 2 dc and around next cluster; YO and draw through all 4 lps on hook—3-FPdc CL made.

5-Back Post Double Crochet Cluster (5-BPdc CL):
Keeping last lp of each st on hook, BPdc around each of next 2 dc, around next cluster, and around each of next 2 dc; YO and draw through all 6 lps on hook—5-BPdc CL made.

5-Front Post Double Crochet Cluster (5-FPdc CL):
Keeping last lp of each st on hook, FPdc around each of next 2 dc, around next cluster, and around each of next 2 dc; YO and draw through all 6 lps on hook—5-FPdc CL made.

Instructions

Foundation ch: multiple of 16 + 2

Row 1 (right side):
Keeping last lp of each dc on hook, dc in 3rd and 4th chs from hook, YO and draw through all 3 lps on hook—beg cluster made; dc in next 5 chs, in next ch work (2 dc, ch 1, 2 dc); dc in next 5 chs; * keeping last lp of each dc on hook, dc in next 5 chs, YO and draw through all 6 lps on hook—5-dc cluster made; dc in next 5 chs, in next ch work (2 dc, ch 1, 2 dc); dc in next 5 chs; rep from * to last 3 chs; keeping last lp of each dc on hook, dc in next 3 chs, YO and draw through all 4 lps on hook—3-dc cluster made. Ch 2, turn.

Row 2:
Sk first cluster, 2-BPdc CL (see Pattern Stitches) over next 2 sts; FPdc (see Pattern Stitches) around each of next 5 dc; in next ch-1 sp work (2 dc, ch 1, 2 dc); FPdc around each of next 5 dc; * 5-BPdc CL (see Pattern Stitches) over next 5 sts; FPdc around each of next 5 dc; in next ch-1 sp work (2 dc, ch 1, 2 dc); FPdc around each of next 5 dc; rep from * to last 3 sts; 3-BPdc CL (see Pattern Stitches) over last 3 sts. Ch 2, turn.

continued

Row 3:

Sk first 3-BPdc CL, 2-FPdc CL (see Pattern Stitches on page 37) over next 2 sts; BPdc (see Pattern Stitches on page 37) around each of next 5 sts; in next ch-1 sp work (2 dc, ch 1, 2 dc); BPdc around each of next 5 sts; * 5-FPdc CL (see Pattern Stitches on page 37) over next 5 sts; BPdc around each of next 5 sts; in next ch-1 sp work (2 dc, ch 1, 2 dc); BPdc around each of next 5 sts; rep from * to last 3 sts; 3-FPdc CL (see Pattern Stitches on page 37) over last 3 sts. Ch 2, turn.

Row 4:

Sk next 3-FPdc CL, 2-BPdc CL over next 2 sts; FPdc around each of next 5 sts; in next ch-1 sp work (2 dc, ch 1, 2 dc); FPdc around each of next 5 sts; * 5-BPdc CL over next 5 sts; FPdc around each of next 5 sts; in next ch-1 sp work (2 dc, ch 1, 2 dc); FPdc around each of next 5 sts; rep from * to last 3 sts; 3-BPdc CL over last 3 sts. Ch 2, turn.

Rep Rows 3 and 4 for desired length. At end of last row, do not ch 2; do not turn.

Finish off.

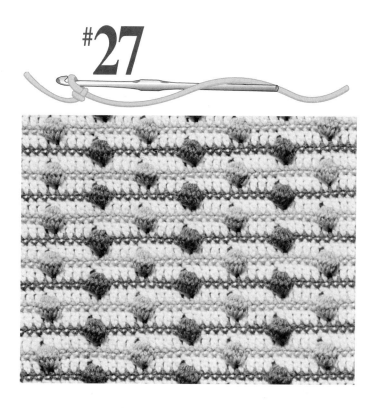

Materials:

Yarn—Color A (off white); Color B (light); Color C (dark)

Pattern Stitch

Cluster (CL):
Keeping last lp of each dc on hook, 5 dc in st indicated; YO and draw through all 6 lps on hook; ch 1—CL made. Push CL to right side.

Instructions

Foundation ch with Color A: multiple of 10 + 3

Row 1 (wrong side):

Sc in 2nd ch from hook and in each rem ch.
Ch 2 (counts as first dc on following rows), turn.

Note: *On following rows, change colors by drawing lp of new color through last lp of old color.*

Row 2 (right side):

Dc in each sc; change to Color B; cut Color A.
Ch 1, turn.

Row 3:

Sc in first 3 dc, CL (see Pattern Stitch) in next dc; * sc in next 9 dc, CL in next dc; rep from * to last 8 sts; sc in last 7 dc and in 2nd ch of turning ch-2; change to Color A; cut Color B. Ch 2, turn.

Row 4:
Dc in each sc and in ch-1 sp of each CL; change to Color C; cut Color A. Ch 1, turn.

Row 5:
Sc in first 8 dc, CL in next dc; * sc in next 9 dc, CL in next dc; rep from * to last 3 sts; sc in next 2 dc and in 2nd ch of turning ch-2; change to Color A; cut Color C. Ch 2, turn.

Row 6:
Dc in each sc and in top of each CL; change to Color B; cut Color A. Ch 1, turn.

Rep Rows 3 through 6 for desired length, ending with Row 4. At end of last row, do not change color. Ch 1, turn.

Last Row:
Sc in each dc to turning ch-2; sc in 2nd ch of turning ch-2.

Finish off.

#28

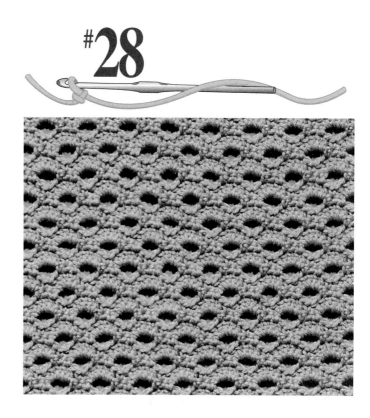

Materials:
Yarn—One color

Instructions
Foundation ch: multiple of 6 + 2

Row 1 (wrong side):
Sc in 2nd ch from hook and in next ch; * ch 3, sk next 3 chs, sc in next 3 chs; rep from * to last 5 chs; ch 3, sk next 3 chs, sc in last 2 chs. Ch 1, turn.

Row 2 (right side):
Sc in first sc; * 5 dc in next ch-3 sp; sk next sc, sc in next sc; rep from * across. Ch 3 (counts as first sc and ch-2 sp on following rows), turn.

Row 3:
Sk next dc, sc in next 3 dc; * ch 3, sk next 3 sts, sc in next 3 dc; rep from * to last 2 sts; ch 2, sk next dc, sc in last sc. Ch 2 (counts as first dc on following rows), turn.

Row 4:
2 dc in next ch-2 sp; sk next sc, sc in next sc; * 5 dc in next ch-3 sp; sk next sc, sc in next sc; rep from * to turning ch-3; 3 dc in sp formed by turning ch-3. Ch 1, turn.

Row 5:
Sc in first 2 dc, ch 3, sk next 3 sts; * sc in next 3 dc, ch 3, sk next 3 sts; rep from * to last 2 sts; sc in next dc and in 2nd ch of turning ch-2. Ch 1, turn.

Rep Rows 2 through 5 for desired length. At end of last row, do not ch 1; do not turn.

Finish off.

#29

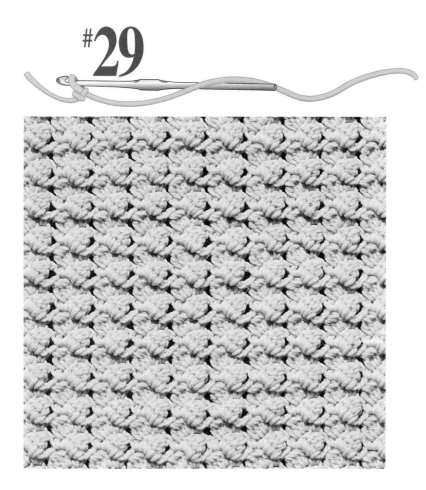

Materials:
Yarn—One color

Pattern Stitch

Cluster (CL):
Keeping last lp of each dc on hook, 4 dc in sp indicated; YO and draw through all 5 lps on hook— CL made.

Instructions

Foundation ch: multiple of 5 + 2

Row 1 (right side):
Sc in 2nd ch from hook; * ch 3, keeping last lp of each dc on hook, dc in next 4 chs, YO and draw through all 5 lps on hook; ch 1, sc in next ch; rep from * across. Ch 3 (counts as first dc and ch-1 sp on following rows), turn.

Row 2:
Sk next ch-1 sp, sc in next st; * ch 3, CL (see Pattern Stitch) in next ch-3 sp; ch 1, sk next sc and next ch-1 sp, sc in next st; rep from * to last ch-3 sp; ch 3, keeping last lp of each dc on hook, 4 dc in last ch-3 sp, dc in last sc; YO and draw through all 6 lps on hook. Ch 1, turn.

Row 3:
Sc in first st, ch 3, CL in next ch-3 sp; ch 1; * sk next sc and next ch-1 sp, sc in next st, ch 3, CL in next ch-3 sp; ch 1; rep from * to last sc; sk last sc and next ch of turning ch-3, sc in next ch. Ch 3, turn.

Rep Rows 2 and 3 for desired length. At end of last row, do not ch 3; do not turn.

Finish off.

#30

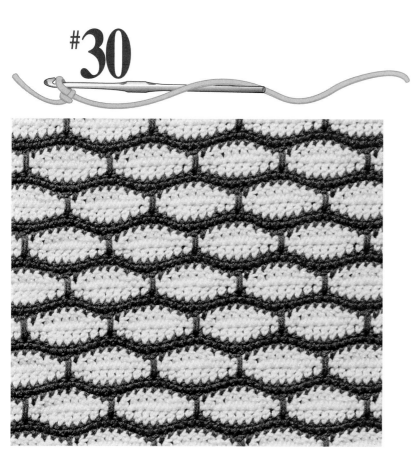

Materials:
Yarn—Color A (dark); Color B (light)

Instructions
Foundation ch with Color A: multiple of 10 + 2

Row 1 (wrong side):
Sc in 2nd ch from hook and in each rem ch; change to Color B by drawing lp through; cut Color A. Ch 1, turn.

Row 2 (right side):
Sc in first 2 sc, hdc in next sc, dc in next 5 sc, hdc in next sc, sc in next sc; * ch 1, sk next sc, sc in next sc, hdc in next sc, dc in next 5 sc, hdc in next sc, sc in next sc; rep from * to last sc; sc in last sc. Ch 1, turn.

Row 3:
Sc in first 2 sc, hdc in next hdc, dc in next 5 dc, hdc in next hdc, sc in next sc; * ch 1, sk next ch-1 sp, sc in next sc, hdc in next hdc, dc in next 5 dc, hdc in next hdc, sc in next sc; rep from * to last sc; sc in last sc; change to Color A by drawing lp through; cut Color B. Ch 1, turn.

Row 4:
Sc in first 10 sts; * working over ch-1 sps of prev 2 rows, dc in skipped sc on 3rd row below; sc in next 9 sts; rep from * to last sc; sc in last sc. Ch 1, turn.

Row 5:
Sc in each st; change to Color B by drawing lp through; cut Color A. Ch 2 (counts as first dc on following rows), turn.

Row 6:
Dc in next 2 sc, hdc in next sc, sc in next sc, ch 1, sk next sc, sc in next sc, hdc in next sc; * dc in next 5 sc, hdc in next sc, sc in next sc, ch 1, sk next sc, sc in next sc, hdc in next sc; rep from * to last 3 sc; dc in last 3 sc. Ch 2, turn.

Row 7:
Dc in next 2 dc, hdc in next hdc, sc in next sc, ch 1, sc in next sc, hdc in next hdc; * dc in next 5 dc, hdc in next hdc, sc in next sc, ch 1, sk next ch-1 sp, sc in next sc, hdc in next hdc; rep from * to last 3 sts; dc in next 2 dc and in 2nd ch of turning ch-2; change to Color A by drawing lp through; cut Color B. Ch 1, turn.

Row 8:
Sc in first 5 sts, working over ch-1 sps of prev 2 rows, dc in skipped sc on 3rd row below; * sc in next 9 sts, working over ch-1 sps of prev 2 rows, dc in skipped sc on 3rd row below; rep from * to last 5 sts; sc in next 4 sts and in 2nd ch of turning ch-2. Ch 1, turn.

Row 9:
Sc in each st; change to Color B by drawing lp through; cut Color A. Ch 1, turn.

Rep Rows 2 through 9 for desired length, ending with Row 4. At end of last row, do not ch 1; do not turn.

Finish off.

#31

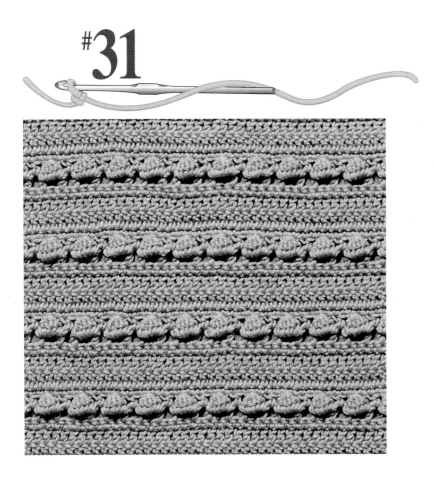

Materials:
Yarn—One color

Pattern Stitch

Cluster (CL):
Keeping last lp of each dc on hook, 5 dc in ch-2 sp indicated; YO and draw through all 6 lps on hook—CL made. Push CL to right side.

Instructions
Foundation ch: multiple of 4

Row 1 (wrong side):
Sc in 2nd ch from hook and in each rem ch. Ch 4 (counts as first hdc and ch-2 sp on following rows), turn.

Row 2 (right side):
Sk next sc, hdc in next sc; * ch 2, sk next sc, hdc in next sc; rep from * across. Ch 2, turn.

Row 3:
* Hdc in next ch-2 sp, ch 1, CL (see Pattern Stitch) in next ch-2 sp; ch 1; rep from * to turning ch-2; sk next ch of turning ch, hdc in next 2 chs. Ch 1, turn.

Row 4:
Sc in each hdc, in each ch, and in each CL to turning ch-2; sc in 2nd ch of turning ch-2. Ch 2, turn.

Row 5:
Dc in each sc. Ch 2, turn.

Row 6:
Dc in each dc to turning ch-2; dc in 2nd ch of turning ch-2. Ch 1, turn.

Row 7:
Sc in each dc to turning ch-2; sc in 2nd ch of turning ch-2. Ch 4, turn.

Rep Rows 2 through 7 for desired length, ending with Row 4. At end of last row, do not ch 2; do not turn.

Finish off.

#32

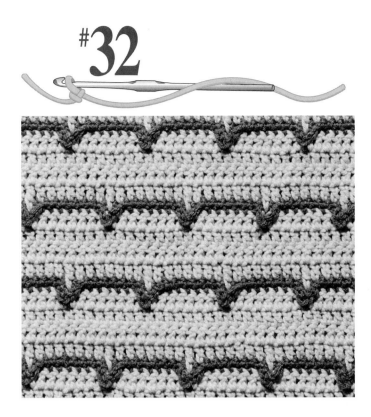

Materials:
Yarn—Color A (light); Color B (dark)

Instructions

Foundation ch with Color A: multiple of 8

Row 1 (right side):
Dc in 3rd ch from hook (2 skipped chs count as a dc) and in each rem ch. Ch 2 (counts as first dc on following rows), turn.

Row 2:
Dc in each dc to beg 2 skipped chs; dc in 2nd ch of beg 2 skipped chs; change to Color B by drawing lp through; cut Color A. Ch 1, turn.

Row 3:
Sc in first 3 dc, ch 3, sc in next dc on 2nd row below (already worked), ch 3, on working row, sk next dc; * sc in next 7 dc, ch 3, sc in next dc on 2nd row below (already worked), ch 3, on working row, sk next dc; rep from * to last 3 sts; sc in last 2 dc and in 2nd ch of turning ch-2. Ch 1, turn.

Row 4:
Sc in first 3 sc, sc in next skipped dc on 2nd row below; * sc in next 7 sc, sc in skipped dc on 2nd row below; rep from * to last 3 sc; sc in last 3 sc; change to Color A by drawing lp through; cut Color B. Ch 2, turn.

Row 5:
Dc in next 2 sc, working over next sc, trc in corresponding dc below (already worked); * on working row, dc in next 7 sc; working over next sc, trc in corresponding dc below (already worked); rep from * to last 3 sc; dc in last 3 sc. Ch 2, turn.

Row 6:
Dc in each st to turning ch-2; dc in 2nd ch of turning ch-2. Ch 2, turn.

Row 7:
Rep Row 6.

Row 8:
Dc in each dc to turning ch-2; dc in 2nd ch of turning ch-2; change to Color B by drawing lp through; cut Color A. Ch 1, turn.

Row 9:
Sc in first 7 dc; * ch 3, sc in next dc on 2nd row below (already worked), ch 3, on working row, sk next dc, sc in next 7 dc; rep from * across, working last dc in 2nd ch of turning ch-2. Ch 1, turn.

Row 10:
Sc in first 7 dc; * sc in next skipped dc on 2nd row below, sc in next 7 sc; rep from * across; change to Color A by drawing lp through; cut Color B. Ch 2, turn.

Row 11:
Dc in next 6 sc; * working over next sc, trc in corresponding dc below (already worked); on working row, dc in next 7 sc; rep from * across. Ch 2, turn.

Rows 12 through 14:
Rep Rows 6 through 8.

Rep Rows 3 through 14 for desired length, ending with Row 6. At end of last row, do not ch 2; do not turn.

Finish off.

#33

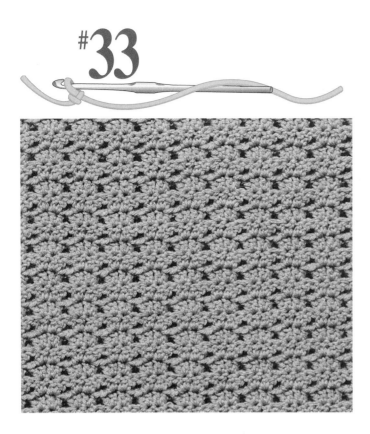

Materials:
Yarn—One color

Instructions

Foundation ch: multiple of 4 + 3

Row 1 (right side):
2 dc in 4th ch from hook (3 skipped chs count as a ch-1 sp and a dc), 2 dc in next ch; * sk next 2 chs, 2 dc in each of next 2 chs; rep from * to last 2 chs; sk next ch, dc in last ch. Ch 2 (counts as first dc on following rows), turn.

Row 2:
Sk next dc, 2 dc in each of next 2 dc; * sk next 2 dc, 2 dc in each of next 2 dc; rep from * to beg 3 skipped chs; dc in 3rd ch of beg 3 skipped chs. Ch 2, turn.

Row 3:
Sk next dc, 2 dc in each of next 2 dc; * sk next 2 dc, 2 dc in each of next 2 dc; rep from * to turning ch-2; dc in 2nd ch of turning ch-2. Ch 2, turn.

Rep Row 3 for desired length. At end of last row, do not ch 2; do not turn.

Finish off.

#34

Materials:
Yarn—One color

Instructions

Foundation ch: multiple of 4 + 2

Row 1 (right side):
Sc in 2nd ch from hook and in each rem ch. Ch 1, turn.

Row 2:
Sc in first sc; * 3 dc in next sc; sk next 2 sc, sc in next sc; rep from * across. Ch 2 (counts as first dc on following rows), turn.

Row 3:
2 dc in first sc; sk next 2 dc, sc in next dc; * 3 dc in next sc; sk next 2 dc, sc in next dc; rep from * to last sc; dc in last sc. Ch 1, turn.

Row 4:
Sc in first dc, 3 dc in next sc; sk next 2 dc; * sc in next dc, 3 dc in next sc, sk next 2 dc; rep from * to turning ch-2; sc in 2nd ch of turning ch-2. Ch 2, turn.

Rep Rows 3 and 4 for desired length. At end of last row, do not ch 2. Ch 1, turn.

Last Row:
Sc in each sc and in each dc.

Finish off.

#35

Materials:
Yarn—One color

Instructions
Foundation ch: multiple of 2 + 1

Row 1 (right side**):**
Sc in 2nd ch from hook and in each rem ch. Ch 1, turn.

Row 2:
Sc in first 2 sc; * ch 4, sl st in 4th ch from hook—picot made; sc in next 2 sc; rep from * across. Ch 1, turn.

Row 3:
Sc in first 2 sc; working behind picots, sc in each sc. Ch 1, turn.

Row 4:
Sc in first sc, picot; * sc in next 2 sc, picot; rep from * to last sc; sc in last sc. Ch 1, turn.

Row 5:
Sc in first sc; working behind picots, sc in each sc. Ch 1, turn.

Rep Rows 2 through 5 for desired length.

Last Row:
Sc in each sc.

Finish off.

#36

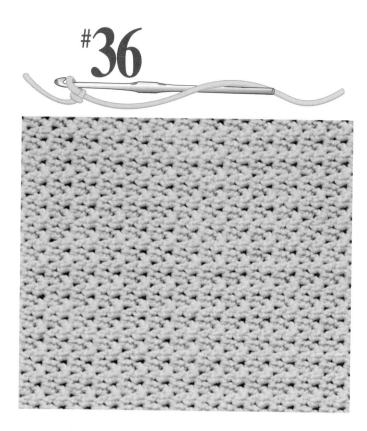

Materials:

Yarn—One color

Instructions

Foundation ch: multiple of 3 + 2

Row 1 (right side):

In 5th ch from hook work (sc, hdc, dc); * sk next 2 chs, in next ch work (sc, hdc, dc); rep from * across to last 3 chs; sk next 2 chs, dc in last ch. Ch 2, turn.

Row 2:

In next dc work (sc, hdc, dc); * sk next 2 sts, in next dc work (sc, hdc, dc); rep from * to beg 4 skipped chs; sk next 2 chs, dc in next ch. Ch 2, turn.

Row 3:

* In next dc work (sc, hdc, dc); sk next 2 sts; rep from * to turning ch-2; dc in 2nd ch of turning ch-2. Ch 2, turn.

Rep Row 3 for desired length. At end of last row, do not ch 2; do not turn.

Finish off.

#37

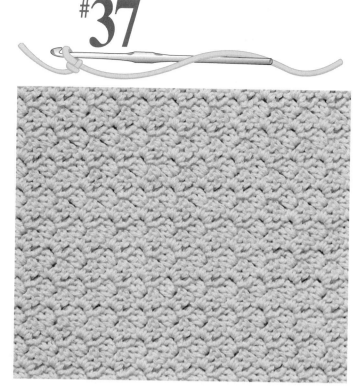

Materials:

Yarn—One color

Instructions

Foundation ch: multiple of 3 + 2

Row 1 (right side):

Sc in 2nd ch from hook and in each rem ch. Ch 1, turn.

Row 2:

In first sc work (sl st, ch 3, 2 dc)—shell made; sk next 2 sc; * in next sc work (sl st, ch 3, 2 dc)—shell made; sk next 2 sc; rep from * to last sc; sc in last sc. Ch 1, turn.

Row 3:

Shell in first sc; * in ch-3 sp of next shell work shell; rep from * to last shell; sc in ch-3 sp of last shell. Ch 1, turn.

Rep Row 3 for desired length. At end of last row, do not ch 1; do not turn.

Finish off.

#38

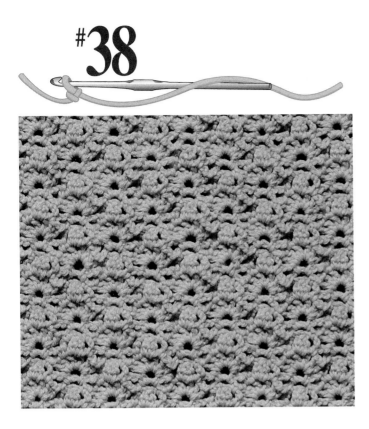

Materials:
Yarn—One color

Pattern Stitch

Cluster (CL):
Keeping last lp of each dc on hook, 3 dc in sp indicated; YO and draw through all 4 lps on hook—CL made.

Instructions
Foundation ch: multiple of 10 + 3

Row 1 (right side):
In 3rd ch from hook (2 skipped chs count as a dc) work (dc, ch 1, dc, ch 1, dc); sk next 3 chs, sc in next ch, ch 3, sk next ch, sc in next ch, sk next 3 chs; * in next ch work (dc, ch 1) 5 times; dc in same ch; sk next 3 chs, sc in next ch, ch 3, sk next ch, sc in next ch, sk next 3 chs; rep from * to last ch; in last ch work (dc, ch 1, dc, ch 1, 2 dc). Ch 2 (counts as first dc on following rows), turn.

Row 2:
Dc in first dc, ch 3, sc in next ch-1 sp, ch 2, sk next ch-1 sp, in next ch-3 sp work (sc, ch 3, sc); ch 2, sk next ch-1 sp, sc in next ch-1 sp, ch 3; * in next ch-1 sp work CL (see Pattern Stitch); ch 3, sc in next ch-1 sp, ch 2,

sk next ch-1 sp, in next ch-3 sp work (sc, ch 3, sc); ch 2, sk next ch-1 sp, sc in next ch-1 sp, ch 3; rep from * to last 2 sts; sk last dc, 2 dc in 2nd ch of beg 2 skipped chs. Ch 3 (counts as first hdc and ch-1 sp on following rows), turn.

Row 3:
Sc in next ch-3 sp, sk next ch-2 sp, in next ch-3 sp work (dc, ch 1) 5 times; dc in same sp; sk next ch-2 sp; * sc in next ch-3 sp, ch 3, sc in next ch-3 sp, sk next ch-2 sp, in next ch-3 sp work (dc, ch 1) 5 times; dc in same sp; sk next ch-2 sp; rep from * to last ch-3 sp; sc in last ch-3 sp, ch 1, sk next dc, hdc in 2nd ch of turning ch-2. Ch 2, turn.

Row 4:
Sc in next ch-1 sp, ch 2, sk next ch-1 sp, sc in next ch-1 sp, ch 3, CL in next ch-1 sp; ch 3, sc in next ch-1 sp, ch 2, sk next ch-1 sp; * in next ch-3 sp work (sc, ch 3, sc); ch 2, sk next ch-1 sp, sc in next ch-1 sp, ch 3, CL in next ch-1 sp; ch 3, sc in next ch-1 sp, ch 2, sk next ch-1 sp; rep from * to turning ch-3; sc in next ch of turning ch, hdc in next ch. Ch 2, turn.

Row 5:
In first hdc work (dc, ch 1, dc, ch 1, dc); sk next ch-2 sp, sc in next ch-3 sp, ch 3, sc in next ch-3 sp, sk next ch-2 sp; * in next ch-3 sp work (dc, ch 1) 5 times; dc in same sp; sk next ch-2 sp, sc in next ch-3 sp, ch 3, sc in next ch-3 sp, sk next ch-2 sp; rep from * to turning ch-2; in 2nd ch of turning ch-2 work (dc, ch 1, dc, ch 1, 2 dc). Ch 2, turn.

Row 6:
Dc in first dc, ch 3, sc in next ch-1 sp, ch 2, sk next ch-1 sp, in next ch-3 sp work (sc, ch 3, sc); ch 2, sk next ch-1 sp, sc in next ch-1 sp, ch 3; * CL in next ch-1 sp; ch 3, sc in next ch-1 sp, ch 2, sk next ch-1 sp, in next ch-3 sp work (sc, ch 3, sc); ch 2, sk next ch-1 sp, sc in next ch-1 sp, ch 3; rep from * to turning ch-2; 2 dc in 2nd ch of turning ch-2. Ch 3, turn.

Rep Rows 3 through 6 for desired length, ending with Row 5. At end of last row, do not ch 2; do not turn.

Finish off.

#39

Materials:
Yarn—Color A (off white); Color B (dark);
Color C (light)

Color Sequence:
4 rows Color A
2 rows Color B
2 rows Color C
end with 4 rows Color A

Instructions
Foundation ch with Color A: multiple of 2 + 1

Row 1 (right side):
YO, insert hook in 3rd ch from hook and draw up lp;
YO, sk next ch, draw up lp in next ch; YO and draw
through all 5 lps on hook; ch 1—eye of st made;
* YO, draw up lp in same ch as last st made; YO,
sk next ch, draw up lp in next ch; YO and draw
through all 5 lps on hook; ch 1—eye of st made; rep
from * across. Ch 2, turn.

Row 2:
YO, draw up lp in eye of first st; YO, draw up lp in eye
of next st; YO and draw through all 5 lps on hook;
ch 1—eye of st made; * YO, draw up lp in eye of same
st as last st made; YO, draw up lp in eye of next st;
YO and draw through all 5 lps on hook; ch 1—eye of
st made; rep from * to beg 2 skipped chs; YO, draw up
lp in eye of same st as last st made; YO, draw up lp in
2nd ch of beg 2 skipped chs; YO and draw through all
5 lps on hook; ch 1—eye of st made. Ch 2, turn.

Row 3:
YO, draw up lp in eye of first st; YO, draw up lp in
eye of next st; YO and draw through all 5 lps on hook;
ch 1—eye of st made; * YO, draw up lp in eye of same
st as last st made; YO, draw up lp in eye of next st;
YO and draw through all 5 lps on hook; ch 1—eye of st
made; rep from * to turning ch-2; YO, draw up lp in
eye of same st as last st made; YO, draw up lp in
2nd ch of turning ch-2; YO and draw through all 5 lps
on hook; ch 1—eye of st made. Ch 2, turn.

Row 4:
Rep Row 3. At end of row, change to next color in
sequence by drawing lp through eye of last st; cut
prev color.

Working in color sequence, rep Row 4 for desired
length. At end of last row, do not ch 2; do not turn.

Finish off.

#40

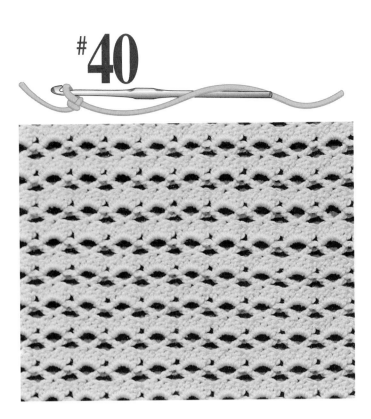

Materials:

Yarn—One color

Instructions

Foundation ch: multiple of 5 + 2

Row 1 (right side):
Sc in 2nd ch from hook; * ch 4, sk next 4 chs, sc in next ch; rep from * across. Ch 2 (counts as first dc on following rows), turn.

Row 2:
* 5 dc in next ch-4 sp—shell made; rep from * to last sc; dc in last sc. Ch 2, turn.

Row 3:
* In 3rd dc of next shell work (dc, ch 3, dc)—V-st made; rep from * to turning ch-2; dc in 2nd ch of turning ch-2. Ch 2, turn.

Row 4:
Shell in ch-3 sp of each V-st; dc in 2nd ch of turning ch-2. Ch 2, turn.

Rep Rows 3 and 4 for desired length. At end of last row, do not ch 2; do not turn.

Finish off.

#41

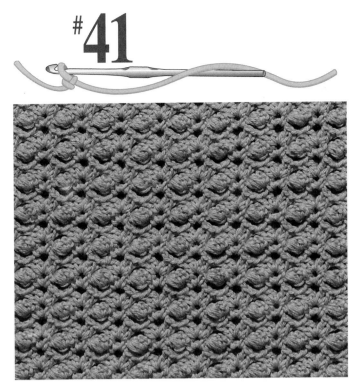

Materials:

Yarn—One color

Pattern Stitch

Puff Stitch (puff st):
Ch 4, YO, draw up lp in 4th ch from hook, (YO, draw up lp in same ch) twice; YO, draw through 6 lps on hook; YO and draw through 2 lps on hook—puff st made.

Instructions

Foundation ch: multiple of 4 + 3

Row 1 (right side):
In 3rd ch from hook work (dc, ch 3, 2 dc); * sk next 3 chs, in next ch work (2 dc, ch 3, 2 dc)—shell made; rep from * across. Ch 1, turn.

Row 2:
In ch-3 sp of next shell work (sc, ch 3, sc)—V-st made; * puff st (see Pattern Stitch); in ch-3 sp of next shell work (sc, ch 3, sc)—V-st made; rep from * across. Ch 1, turn.

Row 3:
Sl st in ch-3 sp of next V-st, ch 3, in same sp work (dc, ch 3, 2 dc)—beg shell made; * sk next puff st, in ch-3 sp of next V-st work (2 dc, ch 3, 2 dc)—shell made; rep from * across. Ch 1, turn.

Rep Rows 2 and 3 for desired length. At end of last row, do not ch 1; do not turn.

Finish off.

#42

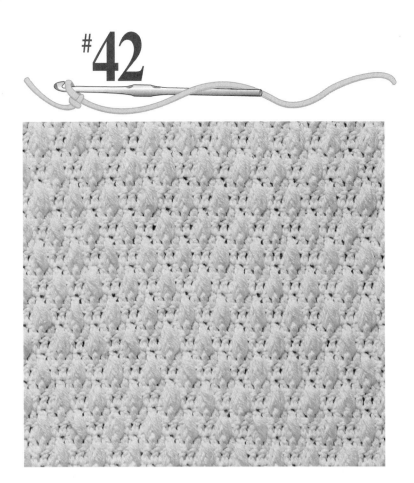

Materials:
Yarn—One color

Pattern Stitch

Twist:

YO, insert hook from front to back to front around post (see page 7) of st indicated on 2nd row below, draw up lp to height of working row, YO, insert hook from front to back to front around post of same dc, draw up lp to height of working row, YO, draw through 4 lps on hook; YO and draw through 2 lps on hook—twist made. **Note:** Sk st behind twist on working row.

Instructions
Foundation ch: multiple of 4 + 2

Row 1 (right side):
Dc in 3rd ch from hook (2 skipped chs count as a dc) and in each rem ch. Ch 2 (counts as first dc on following rows), turn.

Row 2:
Dc in each dc to beg 2 skipped chs; dc in 2nd ch of beg 2 skipped chs. Ch 2, turn.

Row 3:
* Dc in next 3 dc, twist (see Pattern Stitch) around post of next dc on 2nd row below; rep from * to last 4 sts; dc in last 3 dc and in 2nd ch of turning ch-2. Ch 2, turn.

Row 4:
Dc in each dc and in each twist to turning ch-2; dc in 2nd ch of turning ch-2. Ch 2, turn.

Row 5:
Dc in next dc, twist; * dc in next 3 dc, twist; rep from * to last 2 sts; dc in last dc and in 2nd ch of turning ch-2. Ch 2, turn.

Row 6:
Rep Row 4.

Rep Rows 3 through 6 for desired length, ending with Row 3. At end of last row, do not ch 2; do not turn.

Finish off.

#43

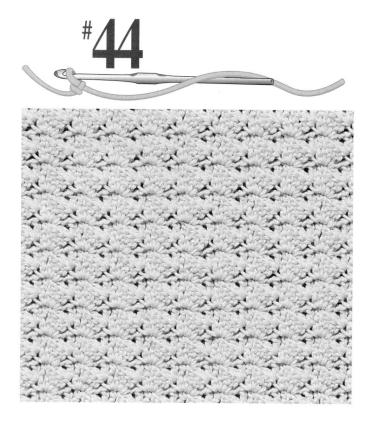

Materials:
Yarn—One color

Instructions

Foundation ch: multiple of 3 + 2

Row 1 (right side):
In 2nd ch from hook work (sc, 2 dc); sk next 2 chs; * in next ch work (sc, 2 dc); sk next 2 chs; rep from * to last ch; sc in last ch. Ch 1, turn.

Row 2:
In first sc work (sc, 2 dc); sk next 2 dc; * in next sc work (sc, 2 dc); sk next 2 dc; rep from * to last sc; sc in last sc. Ch 1, turn.

Rep Row 2 for desired length. At end of last row, do not ch 1; do not turn.

Finish off.

#44

Materials:
Yarn—One color

Instructions

Foundation ch: multiple of 4 + 2

Row 1 (wrong side):
In 2nd ch from hook work (sc, ch 3, 3 dc); * sk next 3 chs, in next ch work (sc, ch 3, 3 dc); rep from * to last 4 chs; sk next 3 chs, sc in last ch. Ch 2 (counts as first dc on following rows), turn.

Row 2 (right side):
Dc in first sc, sc in next ch-3 sp; * in next sc work (dc, ch 1, dc); sc in next ch-3 sp; rep from * to last sc; 2 dc in last sc. Ch 1, turn.

Row 3:
Sc in first dc, sk next dc; * in next sc work (sc, ch 3, 3 dc); rep from * to last 2 sts; sk next dc, sc in 2nd ch of turning ch-2. Ch 2, turn.

Row 4:
Dc in first sc, sc in next ch-3 sp; * in next sc work (dc, ch 1, dc); sc in next ch-3 sp; rep from * to last 2 sc; sk next sc, 2 dc in last sc. Ch 1, turn.

Rep Rows 3 and 4 for desired length. At end of last row, do not ch 1; do not turn.

Finish off.

#45

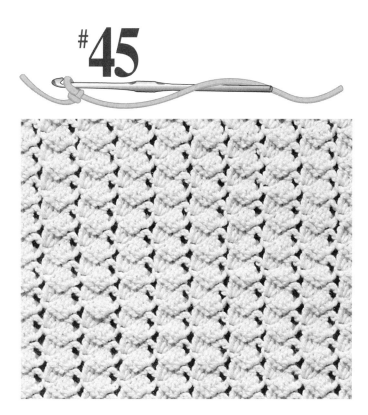

Materials:
Yarn—One color

Instructions
Foundation ch: multiple of 7 + 5

Row 1 (right side):
Sc in 2nd ch from hook, sk next 2 chs, 3 dc in next ch;
* ch 3, sk next 3 chs, sc in next ch, sk next 2 chs, 3 dc in next ch; rep from * across. Ch 1, turn.

Row 2:
Sc in first dc, 3 dc in next sc; * ch 3, sc in next ch-3 sp, 3 dc in next sc; rep from * across. Ch 1, turn.

Rep Row 2 for desired length. At end of last row, do not ch 1; do not turn.

Finish off.

#46

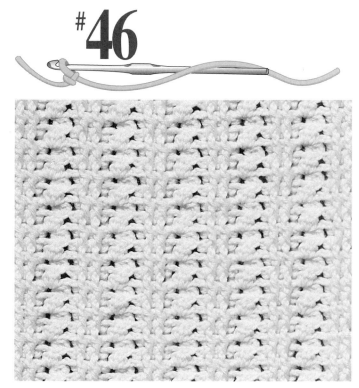

Materials:
Yarn—One color

Pattern Stitches

Cluster (CL):
Keeping last lp of each dc on hook, 3 dc in st or sp indicated; YO and draw through all 4 lps on hook, ch 1—CL made.

Front Post Double Crochet (FPdc):
YO, insert hook from front to back to front around post (see page 7) of next st, YO, draw up lp, (YO, draw through 2 lps on hook) twice—FPdc made.

Back Post Double Crochet (BPdc):
YO, insert hook from back to front to back around post (see page 7) of next st, YO, draw up lp, (YO, draw through 2 lps on hook) twice—BPdc made.

Instructions
Foundation ch: multiple of 8

Row 1 (right side):
In 5th ch from hook (4 skipped chs count as a dc and a ch-2 sp) work CL (see Pattern Stitches); * sk next 2 chs, dc in next 5 chs, ch 2, CL in next ch; rep from * to last 3 chs; sk next 2 chs, dc in last ch. Ch 4 (counts as first dc and ch-2 sp on following rows), turn.

Row 2:
CL in ch-1 sp of next CL; * sk next ch-2 sp, [FPdc (see Pattern Stitches on page 52) around next dc, BPdc (see Pattern Stitches on page 52) around next dc] twice; FPdc around next dc; ch 2, CL in ch-1 sp of next CL; rep from * to beg 4 skipped chs; sk next 2 chs, dc in next ch. Ch 4, turn.

Row 3:
CL in ch-1 sp of next CL; * sk next ch-2 sp, (BPdc around next FPdc, FPdc around next BPdc) twice; BPdc around next FPdc; ch 2, CL in ch-1 sp of next CL; rep from * to turning ch-4; sk next 2 chs of turning ch, dc in next ch. Ch 4, turn.

Row 4:
CL in ch-1 sp of next CL; * (FPdc around next BPdc, BPdc around next FPdc) twice; FPdc around next BPdc; ch 2, CL in ch-1 sp of next CL; rep from * to turning ch-4; sk next 2 chs of turning ch, dc in next ch. Ch 4, turn.

Rep Rows 3 and 4 for desired length, ending with Row 3. At end of last row, do not ch 4; do not turn.

Finish off.

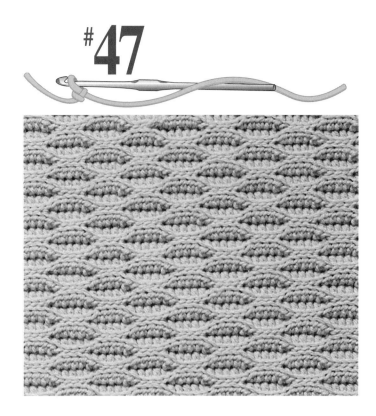

#47

Materials:
Yarn—One color

Instructions
Foundation ch: multiple of 10 + 6

Row 1 (right side):
Sl st in 2nd ch from hook and in next 4 chs; * hdc in next 5 chs, sl st in next 5 chs; rep from * across. Turn.

Note: *Remainder of piece is worked in BLs only.*

Row 2:
Sl st in first 5 sl sts; * hdc in next 5 hdc, sl st in next 5 sl sts; rep from * across. Ch 2 (counts as first hdc on following rows), turn.

Row 3:
Hdc in next 4 sl sts; * sl st in next 5 hdc; hdc in next 5 sl sts; rep from * across. Ch 2, turn.

Row 4:
Hdc in next 4 hdc; * sl st in next 5 sl sts; hdc in next 5 hdc; rep from * across, working last hdc in 2nd ch of turning ch-2. Turn.

Row 5:
Sl st in first 5 hdc; * hdc in next 5 sl sts, sl st in next 5 hdc; rep from * across, working last sl st in 2nd ch of turning ch-2. Turn.

Rep Rows 2 through 5 for desired length. At end of last row, do not turn.

Finish off.

#48

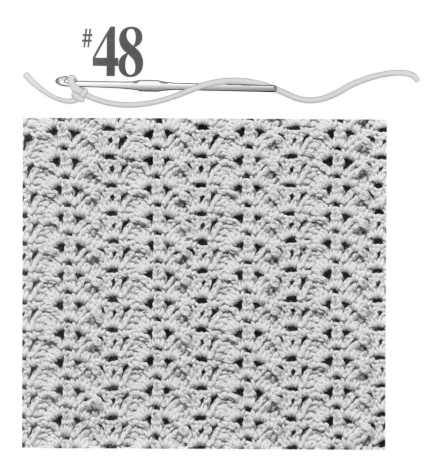

Materials:
Yarn—One color

Pattern Stitch

Cluster (CL):
Keeping last lp of each dc on hook, 2 dc in sp indicated; YO and draw through all 3 lps on hook—CL made.

Instructions
Foundation ch: multiple of 12 + 4

Row 1 (right side):
Sc in 2nd ch from hook, ch 2, sk next ch, sc in next ch; * sk next 3 chs, in next ch work (3 trc, ch 4, sc); ch 2, sk next ch, in next ch work (sc, ch 4, 3 trc); sk next 3 chs, sc in next ch, ch 2, sk next ch, sc in next ch; rep from * across. Ch 3 (counts as first dc and ch-1 sp on following rows), turn.

Row 2:
Dc in next ch-2 sp, ch 1, sk next sc and next 3 trc, sc in next ch-4 sp, ch 2, CL (see Pattern Stitch) in next ch-2 sp; ch 2, sc in next ch-4 sp; * ch 1, in next ch-2 sp work (dc, ch 1) twice; sk next sc and next 3 trc, sc in next ch-4 sp, ch 2, CL in next ch-2 sp; ch 2, sc in next ch-4 sp; rep from * to last ch-2 sp; ch 1, dc in last ch-2 sp, ch 1, dc in last sc. Ch 1, turn.

Row 3:
Sc in first dc, ch 2; * sk next ch-1 sp, sc in next ch-1 sp, in next ch-2 sp work (3 trc, ch 4, sc); ch 2, sk next CL, in next ch-2 sp work (sc, ch 4, 3 trc); sc in next ch-1 sp, ch 2; rep from * to turning ch-3; sk next ch of turning ch, sc in next ch. Ch 3, turn.

Rep Rows 2 and 3 for desired length, ending with Row 2. At end of last row, do not ch 1; do not turn.

Finish off.

#49

Materials:
Yarn—One color

Pattern Stitches

Cluster (CL):
Keeping last lp of each dc on hook, 3 dc in st indicated; YO and draw through all 4 lps on hook—CL made.

2-Double Crochet Cluster (2-dc CL):
Keeping last lp of each dc on hook, dc in next dc, sk next CL, dc in next dc; YO and draw through all 3 lps on hook—2-dc CL made.

Instructions
Foundation ch: multiple of 10 + 3

Row 1 (right side):
2 dc in 3rd ch from hook (beg 2 skipped chs count as a dc); ch 3, sk next 4 chs, sc in next ch, ch 3, sk next 4 chs; * 5 dc in next ch; ch 3, sk next 4 chs, sc in next ch, ch 3, sk next 4 chs; rep from * to last ch; 3 dc in last ch. Ch 3 (counts as first dc and ch-1 sp on following rows), turn.

Row 2:
(Dc in next dc, ch 1) twice; CL (see Pattern Stitches) in next sc; ch 1; * (dc in next dc, ch 1) 5 times; CL in next sc; ch 1; rep from * to last 3 sts; (dc in next dc, ch 1) twice; dc in 2nd ch of beg 2 skipped chs. Ch 4 (counts as first dc and ch-2 sp on following rows), turn.

Row 3:
Dc in next dc, ch 2, 2-dc CL (see Pattern Stitches); ch 2, * (dc in next dc, ch 2) 3 times; 2-dc CL; ch 2; rep from * to last dc; dc in last dc, ch 2, sk next ch of turning ch-3, dc in next ch. Ch 1, turn.

Row 4:
Sc in first dc, ch 1; * sc in next ch-2 sp, ch 3; rep from * to turning ch-4; sc in next ch of turning ch, ch 1, sk next ch, sc in next ch. Ch 2, turn.

Row 5:
2 dc in first sc; ch 3, sk next ch-3 sp, sc in next ch-3 sp, ch 3, sk next ch-3 sp; * 5 dc in next ch-3 sp; ch 3, sk next ch-3 sp, sc in next ch-3 sp, ch 3, sk next ch-3 sp; rep from * to last 2 sc; sk next sc, 3 dc in last sc. Ch 3, turn.

Rep Rows 2 through 5 for desired length, ending with Row 3. At end of last row, do not ch 3; do not turn.

Finish off.

#50

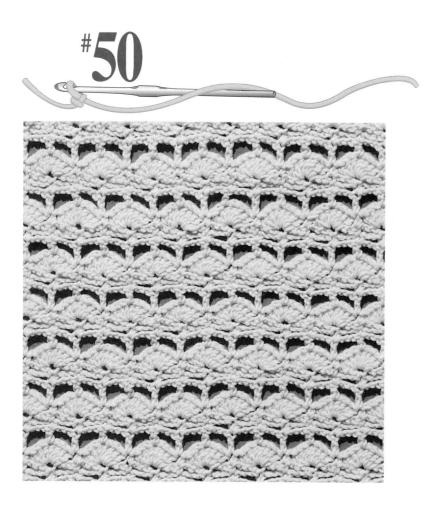

Materials:
Yarn—One color

Instructions
Foundation ch: multiple of 8 + 3

Row 1 (right side):
3 dc in 3rd ch from hook (2 skipped chs count as a dc); sk next 3 chs, sc in next ch; * sk next 3 chs, 7 dc in next ch; sk next 3 chs, sc in next ch; rep from * to last 4 chs; sk next 3 chs, 4 dc in last ch. Ch 5 (counts as first dc and ch-3 sp on following rows), turn.

Row 2:
Sk next 3 dc; * dc in next sc, ch 3, sk next 3 dc, dc in next dc, ch 3, sk next 3 dc; rep from * to last sc; dc in last sc, ch 3, sk next 3 dc, dc in 2nd ch of beg 2 skipped chs. Ch 1, turn.

Row 3:
Sc in first dc, ch 3; * sc in next dc, ch 3; rep from * to turning ch-5; sk next 3 chs of turning ch, sc in next ch. Ch 1, turn.

Row 4:
Sc in first sc; * ch 3, sc in next sc; rep from * across. Ch 1, turn.

Row 5:
Sc in first sc; * 7 dc in next sc; sc in next sc; rep from * across. Ch 5, turn.

Row 6:
Sk next 3 dc, dc in next dc, ch 3, sk next 3 dc, dc in next sc; * ch 3, sk next 3 dc, dc in next dc, ch 3, sk next 3 dc, dc in next sc; rep from * across. Ch 1, turn.

Row 7:
Rep Row 3.

Row 8:
Sc in first sc; * ch 3, sc in next sc; rep from * across. Ch 2, turn.

Row 9:
3 dc in first sc; sc in next sc; * 7 dc in next sc; sc in next sc; rep from * to last sc; 4 dc in last sc. Ch 5, turn.

Row 10:
Sk next 3 dc; * dc in next sc, ch 3, sk next 3 dc, dc in next dc, ch 3; rep from * across to last sc; dc in last sc, ch 3, sk next 3 dc, dc in 2nd ch of turning ch-2. Ch 1, turn.

Rep Rows 3 through 10 for desired length, ending with Row 9. At end of last row, do not ch 5; do not turn.

Finish off.

#51

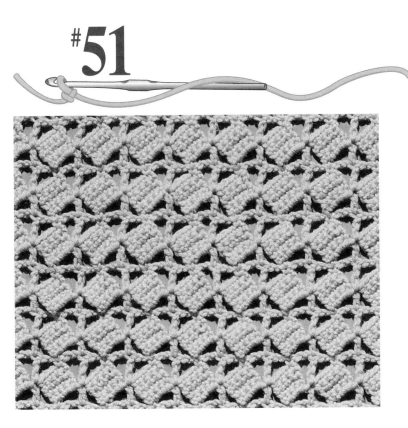

Materials
Yarn—One color

Instructions
Foundation ch: multiple of 6

Row 1 (right side):
Sc in 9th ch from hook (8 skipped chs count as a ch-3 sp, a dc, and a ch-3 sp), ch 1, turn; sc in sc just made, 3 sc in next ch-3 sp; (ch 1, turn; sc in next 4 sc) 3 times; sk next 2 chs of beg ch, dc in next ch; * ch 3, sk next 2 chs, sc in next ch, ch 1, turn; sc in sc just made, 3 sc in next ch-3 sp;(ch 1, turn; sc in next 4 sc) 3 times; sk next 2 chs of beg ch, dc in next ch; rep from * across. Ch 5 (counts as a trc and ch-2 sp on following row), turn.

Row 2:
Sk first dc and next 3 sc, sc in next sc, ch 2, trc in next dc; * ch 2, sk next 3 sc, sc in next sc, ch 2, trc in next dc; rep from * across, working last trc in sp formed by beg 8 skipped chs. Ch 5 (counts as a dc and ch-3 sp on following row), turn.

Row 3:
Sc in next sc, ch 1, turn; sc in sc just made, 3 sc in next ch-3 sp; (ch 1, turn; sc in next 4 sc) 3 times; * dc in next trc, ch 3, sc in next sc, ch 1, turn; sc in sc just made, 3 sc in next ch-3 sp; (ch 1, turn; sc in next 4 sc) 3 times; rep from * to turning ch-5; sk next 2 chs of turning ch, dc in next ch. Ch 5 (counts as a trc and ch-2 sp on following row), turn.

Row 4:
Sk first dc and next 3 sc, sc in next sc, ch 2, trc in next dc; * ch 2, sk next 3 sc, sc in next sc, ch 2, trc in next dc; rep from * across, working last trc in sp formed by turning ch-5. Ch 5 (counts as a dc and ch-3 sp on following row), turn.

Rep Rows 3 and 4 for desired length. At end of last row, do not ch 5; do not turn.

Finish off.

#52

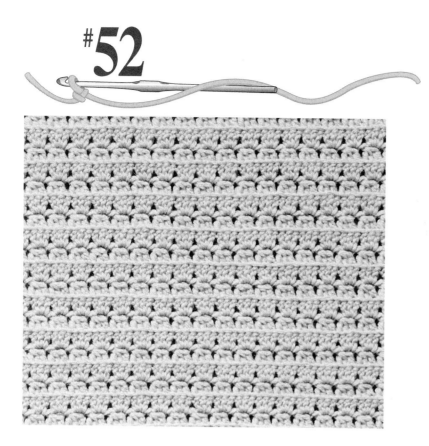

Materials:
Yarn—One color

Pattern Stitch

Cluster (CL):
Keeping last lp of each dc on hook, dc in 3 sts indicated; YO and draw through all 4 lps on hook—CL made.

Instructions
Foundation ch: multiple of 3 + 1

Row 1 (wrong side):
3 dc in 3rd ch from hook (beg 2 skipped chs count as a dc); ∗ sk next 2 chs, 3 dc in next ch; rep from ∗ to last ch; dc in last ch. Ch 2 (counts as first dc on following rows), turn.

Row 2 (right side):
Working in BLs only, CL (see Pattern Stitch) over next 3 dc; ∗ ch 1, CL over next 3 dc; rep from ∗ to beg 2 skipped chs; dc in 2nd ch of beg 2 skipped chs. Ch 2, turn.

Row 3:
Working through both lps, 3 dc in top of first CL; ∗ sk next ch-1 sp, 3 dc in top of next CL; rep from ∗ to turning ch-2; dc in 2nd ch of turning ch-2. Ch 2, turn.

Row 4:
Working in BLs only, CL over next 3 dc; ∗ ch 1, CL over next 3 dc; rep from ∗ to turning ch-2; dc in 2nd ch of turning ch-2. Ch 2, turn.

Rep Rows 3 and 4 for desired length. At end of last row, do not ch 2; do not turn.

Finish off.

#53

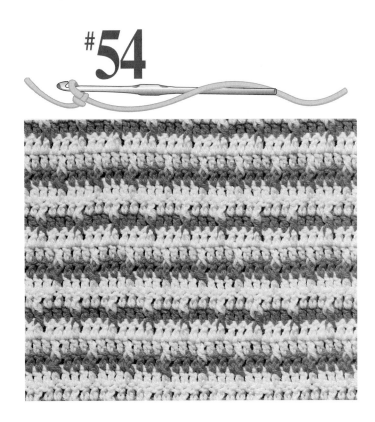

Materials:
Yarn—One color

Instructions
Foundation ch: multiple of 2

Row 1 (right side):
Dc in 3rd ch from hook (2 skipped chs count as a dc) and in each rem ch. Turn.

Row 2:
Sl st in first dc, dc in next dc; * sl st in next dc, dc in next dc; rep from * to beg 2 skipped chs; sl st in 2nd ch of beg 2 skipped chs. Ch 2 (counts as first dc on following rows), turn.

Row 3:
Dc in each dc and in each sl st. Turn.

Row 4:
Sl st in first dc, dc in next dc; * sl st in next dc, dc in next dc; rep from * to turning ch-2; sl st in 2nd ch of turning ch-2. Ch 2, turn.

Row 5:
Dc in each dc and in each sl st. Turn.

Rep Rows 4 and 5 for desired length. At end of last row, do not ch 2; do not turn.

Finish off.

#54

Materials:
Yarn—Color A (light); Color B (dark)

> ### Pattern Stitches
>
> **Front Post Double Crochet** (FPdc):
> YO, insert hook from front to back to front around post (see page 7) of st indicated, draw up lp, (YO, draw through 2 lps on hook) twice— FPdc made.
>
> **Back Post Double Crochet** (BPdc):
> YO, insert hook from back to front to back around post (see page 7) of st indicated, draw up lp, (YO, draw through 2 lps on hook) twice—BPdc made.

Instructions
Foundation ch with Color A: multiple of 4 + 2

Row 1 (right side):
Dc in 3rd ch from hook (2 skipped chs count as a dc) and in each rem ch. Ch 2 (counts as first dc on following rows), turn.

Row 2:
Dc in each dc to beg 2 skipped chs; dc in 2nd ch of beg 2 skipped chs; change to Color B by drawing lp through; cut Color A. Ch 2, turn.

continued

Row 3:
Dc in next dc, FPdc (see Pattern Stitches) around next dc; * dc in next 3 dc, FPdc around next dc; rep from * to last 2 sts; dc in next dc and in 2nd ch of turning ch-2; change to Color A by drawing lp through; cut Color B. Ch 2, turn.

Row 4:
Dc in next dc, BPdc (see Pattern Stitches) around next FPdc; * dc in next 3 dc, BPdc around next FPdc; rep from * to last 2 sts; dc in next dc and in 2nd ch of turning ch-2. Ch 2, turn.

Row 5:
Dc in each st to turning ch-2; dc in 2nd ch of turning ch-2; change to Color B by drawing lp through; cut Color A. Ch 2, turn.

Row 6:
Dc in next 3 dc; * BPdc around next dc; dc in next 3 dc; rep from * to turning ch-2; dc in 2nd ch of turning ch-2; change to Color A by drawing lp through; cut Color B. Ch 2, turn.

Row 7:
Dc in next 3 dc; * FPdc around next BPdc; dc in next 3 dc; rep from * to turning ch-2; dc in 2nd ch of turning ch-2. Ch 2, turn.

Row 8:
Dc in each st to turning ch-2; dc in 2nd ch of turning ch-2; change to Color B by drawing lp through; cut Color A. Ch 2, turn.

Rep Rows 3 through 8 for desired length. At end of last row, do not ch 2; do not turn.

Finish off.

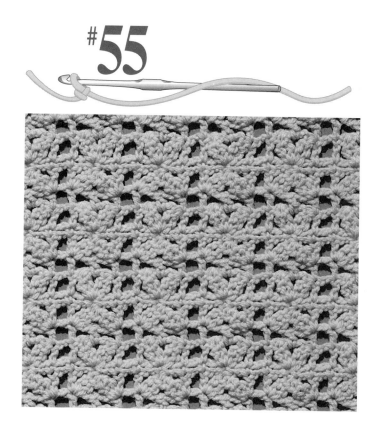

#55

Materials:
Yarn—One color

Pattern Stitches

Cluster (CL):
Keeping last lp of each trc on hook, 2 trc in same st as last dc made; sk next dc, 2 trc in next dc; YO and draw through all 5 lps on hook—CL made.

2-Triple Crochet Cluster (2-trc CL):
Keeping last lp of each trc on hook, 2 trc in st indicated; YO and draw through all 3 lps on hook—2-trc CL made.

Instructions
Foundation ch: multiple of 9 + 7

Row 1 (right side):
Dc in 3rd ch from hook (2 skipped chs count as a dc); * ch 2, sk next 2 chs, dc in next ch; rep from * to last ch; dc in last ch. Ch 2 (counts as first dc on following rows), turn.

Row 2:
Dc in next dc, ch 2, dc in next dc; * ch 2, CL (see Pattern Stitches); ch 2, dc in same st as last 2 trc made; ch 2, dc in next dc; rep from * to beg 2 skipped chs; dc in 2nd ch of beg 2 skipped chs. Ch 1, turn.

Row 3:
Sc in first 2 dc, ch 2, sc in next dc; * ch 2, sc in next CL, (ch 2, sc in next dc) twice; rep from * to turning ch-2; sc in 2nd ch of turning ch-2. Ch 2, turn.

Row 4:
Dc in next sc, ch 2; * dc in next sc, in next sc work [2-trc CL (see Pattern Stitches), ch 3, 2-trc CL]; dc in next sc, ch 2; rep from * to last 2 sc; dc in last 2 sc. Ch 2, turn.

Row 5:
Dc in next dc, ch 2, dc in next dc; * ch 2, dc in next ch-3 sp, (ch 2, dc in next dc) twice; rep from * to turning ch-2; dc in 2nd ch of turning ch-2. Ch 2, turn.

Rep Rows 2 through 5 for desired length. At end of last row, do not ch 2; do not turn.

Finish off.

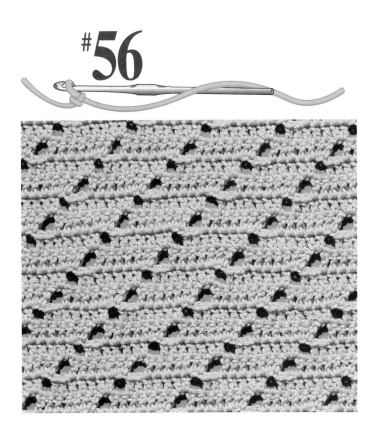

#56

Materials:
Yarn—One color

Instructions
Foundation ch: multiple of 9 + 2

Row 1 (right side):
Dc in 3rd ch from hook (2 skipped chs count as a dc) and in next 2 chs, ch 2, sk next 2 chs; * dc in next 7 chs, ch 2, sk next 2 chs; rep from * to last 4 chs; dc in last 4 chs. Ch 2 (counts as first dc on following rows), turn.

Row 2:
Dc in next 3 dc and in next 2 chs, ch 2, sk next 2 dc; * dc in next 5 dc and in next 2 chs, ch 2, sk next 2 dc; rep from * to last 2 sts; dc in next dc and in 2nd ch of beg 2 skipped chs. Ch 3 (counts as first dc and ch-1 sp on following rows), turn.

Row 3:
Sk next dc, dc in next 2 chs and in next 5 dc; * ch 2, sk next 2 dc, dc in next 2 chs and in next 5 dc; rep from * to turning ch-2; dc in 2nd ch of turning ch-2. Ch 4 (counts as first dc and ch-2 sp on following rows), turn.

Row 4:
Sk next 2 dc, dc in next 5 dc; * dc in next 2 chs, ch 2, sk next 2 dc, dc in next 5 dc; rep from * to turning ch-3; dc in next 2 chs of turning ch-3. Ch 2, turn.

continued

Row 5:
Dc in next 4 dc, ch 2, sk next 2 dc; * dc in next 2 chs and in next 5 dc, ch 2, sk next 2 dc; rep from * to turning ch-4; dc in next 3 chs of turning ch-4. Ch 2, turn.

Row 6:
Dc in next 2 dc and in next 2 chs, ch 2, sk next 2 dc; * dc in next 5 dc and in next 2 chs, ch 2, sk next 2 dc; rep from * to last 3 sts; dc in next 2 dc and in 2nd ch of turning ch-2. Ch 4, turn.

Row 7:
Sk next 2 dc, dc in next 2 chs and in next 5 dc; * ch 2, sk next 2 dc, dc in next 2 chs and in next 5 dc; rep from * across, working last dc in 2nd ch of turning ch-2. Ch 3, turn.

Row 8:
Sk next dc, dc in next 5 dc; * dc in next 2 chs, ch 2, sk next 2 dc, dc in next 5 dc; rep from * to turning ch-4; dc in next 3 chs of turning ch-4. Ch 2, turn.

Row 9:
Dc in next 5 dc, ch 2, sk next 2 dc; * dc in next 2 chs and in next 5 dc, ch 2, sk next 2 dc; rep from * to turning ch-3; dc in next 2 chs of turning ch-3. Ch 2, turn.

Row 10:
Dc in next dc and in next 2 chs, ch 2, sk next 2 dc; * dc in next 5 dc and in next 2 chs, ch 2, sk next 2 dc; rep from * to last 4 sts; dc in next 3 dc and in 2nd ch of turning ch-2. Ch 2, turn.

Row 11:
Dc in next dc, ch 2, sk next 2 dc, dc in next 2 chs; * dc in next 5 dc, ch 2, sk next 2 dc, dc in next 2 chs; rep from * to last 4 dc; dc in next 3 dc and in 2nd ch of turning ch-2. Ch 2, turn.

Row 12:
Dc in next 5 dc and in next 2 chs; * ch 2, sk next 2 dc, dc in next 5 dc and in next 2 chs; rep from * to last 2 sts; ch 1, sk next dc, dc in 2nd ch of turning ch-2. Ch 2, turn.

Row 13:
Dc in next ch and in next 5 dc, ch 2, sk next 2 dc; * dc in next 2 chs and in next 5 dc, ch 2, sk next 2 dc; rep from * to turning ch-2; dc in 2nd ch of turning ch-2. Ch 2, turn.

Row 14:
* Dc in next 2 chs, ch 2, sk next 2 dc, dc in next 5 dc; rep from * across, working last dc in 2nd ch of turning ch-2. Ch 2, turn.

Row 15:
Dc in next 2 dc, ch 2, sk next 2 dc, dc in next 2 chs; * dc in next 5 dc, ch 2, sk next 2 dc, dc in next 2 chs; rep from * to last 3 sts; dc in next 2 dc and in 2nd ch of turning ch-2. Ch 2, turn.

Row 16:
Dc in next 4 dc and in next 2 chs, ch 2, sk next 2 dc; * dc in next 5 dc and in next 2 chs, ch 2, sk next 2 dc; rep from * to turning ch-2; dc in 2nd ch of turning ch-2. Ch 2, turn.

Row 17:
Dc in next 2 chs and in next 5 dc; * ch 2, sk next 2 dc, dc in next 2 chs and in next 5 dc; rep from * to last 2 sts; ch 1, sk next dc, dc in 2nd ch of turning ch-2. Ch 2, turn.

Row 18:
Dc in next ch, ch 2, sk next 2 dc, dc in next 5 dc; * dc in next 2 chs, ch 2, sk next 2 dc, dc in next 5 dc; rep from * to turning ch-2; dc in 2nd ch of turning ch-2. Ch 2, turn.

Row 19:
Dc in next 3 dc, ch 2, sk next 2 dc, dc in next 2 chs; * dc in next 5 dc, ch 2, sk next 2 dc, dc in next 2 chs; rep from * to last 2 sts; dc in next dc and in 2nd ch of turning ch-2. Ch 2, turn.

Row 20:
Dc in next 3 dc and in next 2 chs, ch 2, sk next 2 dc; * dc in next 5 dc and in next 2 chs, ch 2, sk next 2 dc; rep from * to last 2 sts; dc in next dc and in 2nd ch of turning ch-2. Ch 3, turn.

Rep Rows 3 through 20 for desired length, ending with Row 19. At end of last row, do not ch 2; do not turn.

Finish off.

#57

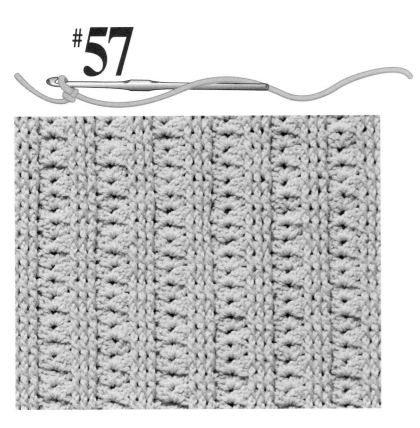

Materials:
Yarn—One color

Pattern Stitches

Front Post Double Crochet (FPdc):
YO, insert hook from front to back to front around post (see page 7) of st indicated, draw up lp, (YO, draw through 2 lps on hook) twice—FPdc made.

Back Post Double Crochet (BPdc):
YO, insert hook from back to front to back around post (see page 7) of st indicated, draw up lp, (YO, draw through 2 lps on hook) twice—BPdc made.

Instructions
Foundation ch: multiple of 8 + 4

Row 1 (wrong side):
Dc in 3rd ch from hook (2 skipped chs count as a dc) and in next ch; * sk next 2 chs, in next ch work (2 dc, ch 1, 2 dc)—shell made; sk next 2 chs, dc in next 3 chs; rep from * across. Ch 2 (counts as first dc on following rows), turn.

Row 2 (right side):
FPdc (see Pattern Stitches) around each of next 2 dc; in ch-1 sp of next shell work shell; sk next 2 dc of same shell; * FPdc around each of next 3 dc; in ch-1 sp of next shell work shell; sk next 2 dc of same shell; rep from * to last 3 sts; FPdc around each of next 2 dc; dc in 2nd ch of beg 2 skipped chs. Ch 2, turn.

Row 3:
BPdc (see Pattern Stitches) around each of next 2 FPdc; shell in next shell; * BPdc around each of next 3 FPdc; shell in next shell; rep from * to last 3 sts; BPdc around each of next 2 FPdc; dc in 2nd ch of turning ch-2. Ch 2, turn.

Row 4:
FPdc around each of next 2 BPdc; shell in next shell; * FPdc around each of next 3 BPdc; shell in next shell; rep from * to last 3 sts; FPdc around each of next 2 BPdc; dc in 2nd ch of turning ch-2. Ch 2, turn.

Rep Rows 3 and 4 for desired length. At end of last row, do not ch 2; do not turn.

Finish off.

#58

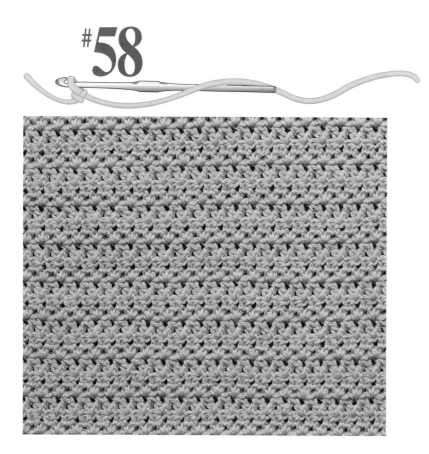

Materials:
Yarn—One color

Instructions
Foundation ch: multiple of 2 + 1

Row 1 (right side**):**
Keeping last lp of each dc on hook, dc in 3rd ch from hook, sk next ch, dc in next ch, YO and draw through all 3 lps on hook; * ch 1, keeping last lp of each dc on hook, dc in same ch as last dc made, sk next ch, dc in next ch, YO and draw through all 3 lps on hook; rep from * across; ch 1, dc in same ch as last dc made. Ch 2, turn.

Row 2:
Keeping last lp of each dc on hook, dc in next ch, sk next st, dc in next ch, YO and draw through all 3 lps on hook—cluster made; * ch 1, keeping last lp of each dc on hook, dc in same ch as last dc made, sk next st, dc in next ch, YO and draw through all 3 lps on hook—cluster made; rep from * across, working last dc of last cluster in 2nd ch of turning ch-2; ch 1, dc in same ch as last dc made. Ch 2, turn.

Row 3:
Keeping last lp of each dc on hook, dc in next ch, sk next cluster, dc in next ch, YO and draw through all 3 lps on hook—cluster made; * ch 1, keeping last lp of each dc on hook, dc in same ch as last dc made, sk next cluster, dc in next ch, YO and draw through all 3 lps on hook—cluster made; rep from * across, working last dc of last cluster in 2nd ch of turning ch-2; ch 1, dc in same ch as last dc made. Ch 2, turn.

Rep Row 3 for desired length. At end of last row, do not ch 2; do not turn.

Finish off.

#59

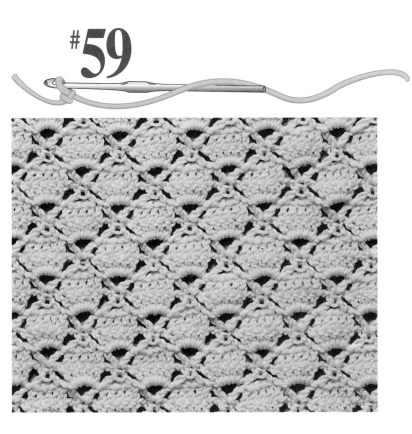

Materials:
Yarn—One color

Pattern Stitches

Cluster (CL):
Keeping last lp of each dc on hook, dc in next dc, sk next 3 dc, dc in next dc; YO and draw through all 3 lps on hook—CL made.

2-Double Crochet Cluster (2-dc CL):
Keeping last lp of each dc on hook, dc in next dc, sk next dc, dc in 2nd ch of turning ch-2; YO and draw through all 3 lps on hook—2-dc CL made.

Instructions
Foundation ch: multiple of 10 + 2

Row 1 (right side):
Dc in 3rd ch from hook (2 skipped chs count as a dc) and in next ch, sk next 2 chs, in next ch work (dc, ch 3, dc)—V-st made; sk next 2 chs; * dc in next 5 chs, sk next 2 chs, in next ch work (dc, ch 3, dc)—V-st made; sk next 2 chs; rep from * to last 3 chs; dc in last 3 chs. Ch 2 (counts as first dc on following rows), turn.

Row 2:
Sk next dc, dc in next dc, ch 2, 5 dc in ch-3 sp of next V-st; ch 2, sk next dc of same V-st; * CL (see Pattern Stitches) over next 5 dc; ch 2, 5 dc in ch-3 sp of next V-st; ch 2, sk next dc of same V-st; rep from * to last 3 sts; 2-dc CL (see Pattern Stitches) over last 3 sts. Ch 3 (counts as first dc and ch-1 sp on following rows), turn.

Row 3:
Dc in first 2-dc CL and in next 5 dc; * V-st in next CL; dc in next 5 dc; rep from * to last ch-2 sp; sk next ch-2 sp and next dc, in 2nd ch of turning ch-2 work (dc, ch 1, dc). Ch 2, turn.

Row 4:
2 dc in first ch-1 sp; ch 2, sk next dc, CL over next 5 dc; ch 2; * 5 dc in ch-3 sp of next V-st; ch 2, sk next dc of same V-st, CL over next 5 dc; ch 2; rep from * to turning ch-3; 3 dc in sp formed by turning ch-3. Ch 2, turn.

Row 5:
Dc in next 2 dc, V-st in next CL; * dc in next 5 dc, V-st in next CL; rep from * to last 3 sts; dc in next 2 dc and in 2nd ch of turning ch-2. Ch 2, turn.

Rep Rows 2 through 5 for desired length, ending with Row 4. At end of last row, do not ch 2; do not turn.

Finish off.

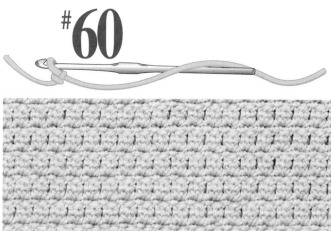

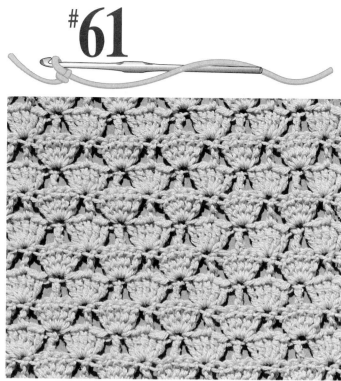

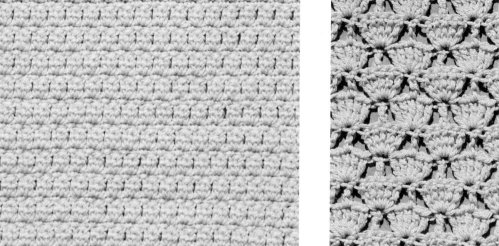

Materials:
Yarn—One color

Pattern Stitch

Cluster (CL):
Keeping last lp of each dc on hook, 3 dc in st indicated; YO and draw through all 4 lps on hook—CL made.

Instructions
Foundation ch: multiple of 2

Row 1 (right side):
Sc in 2nd ch from hook and in each rem ch.
Ch 2 (counts as first dc on following rows), turn.

Row 2:
CL (see Pattern Stitch) in next sc; * ch 1, sk next sc, CL in next sc; rep from * to last sc; dc in last sc.
Ch 1, turn.

Row 3:
Sc in first dc and in each CL and in each ch-1 sp to turning ch-2; sc in 2nd ch of turning ch-2. Ch 2, turn.

Rep Rows 2 and 3 for desired length. At end of last row, do not ch 2; do not turn.

Finish off.

Materials:
Yarn—One color

Instructions
Foundation ch: multiple of 8 + 3

Row 1 (right side):
5 trc in 7th ch from hook (6 skipped chs count as a ch-3 sp and a trc); sk next 3 chs, trc in next ch;
* sk next 3 chs, 5 trc in next ch; sk next 3 chs, trc in next ch; rep from * across. Ch 3 (counts as first trc on following rows), turn.

Row 2:
2 trc in first trc; * sk next 2 trc, trc in next trc, sk next 2 trc, 5 trc in next trc; rep from * to last 5-trc group; sk next 2 trc, trc in next trc, sk next 2 trc, 3 trc in 6th ch of beg 6 skipped chs. Ch 3, turn.

Row 3:
Sk next 2 trc, 5 trc in next trc; * sk next 2 trc, trc in next trc, sk next 2 trc, 5 trc in next trc; rep from * to last 3 sts; sk next 2 trc, trc in 3rd ch of turning ch-3. Ch 3, turn.

Row 4:
2 trc in first trc; * sk next 2 trc, trc in next trc, sk next 2 trc, 5 trc in next trc; rep from * to last 5 sts; sk next 2 trc, trc in next trc, sk next 2 trc, 3 trc in 3rd ch of turning ch-3. Ch 3, turn.

Rep Rows 3 and 4 for desired length, ending with Row 3. At end of last row, do not ch 3; do not turn.

Finish off.

#62

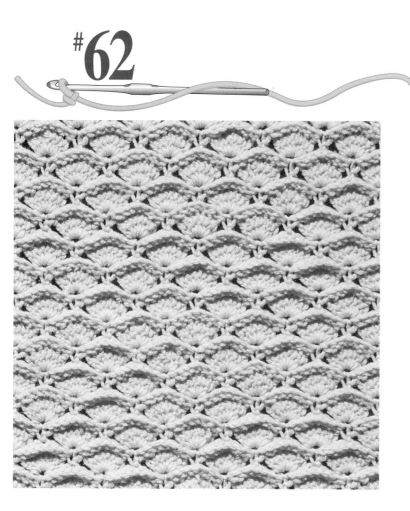

Materials:
Yarn—One color

Pattern Stitch

Back Post Single Crochet (BPsc):
Insert hook from back to front to back around post (see page 7) of st indicated, draw up lp, YO and draw through 2 lps on hook—BPsc made.

Instructions
Foundation ch: multiple of 8 + 2

Row 1 (wrong side):
Sc in 2nd ch from hook; * sk next 3 chs, 7 trc in next ch; sk next 3 chs, sc in next ch; rep from * across. Ch 1, turn.

Row 2 (right side):
Sc in first sc; * BPsc (see Pattern Stitch) around each of next 7 trc; sc in next sc; rep from * across. Ch 3 (counts as first trc on following rows), turn.

Row 3:
3 trc in first sc; sk next 3 sts, sc in next st, sk next 3 sts; * 7 trc in next sc; sk next 3 sts, sc in next st, sk next 3 sts; rep from * to last sc; 4 trc in last sc. Ch 1, turn.

Row 4:
Sc in first trc, BPsc around each of next 3 trc; sc in next sc; * BPsc around each of next 7 trc; sc in next sc; rep from * to last 4 sts; BPsc around each of next 3 trc; sc in 3rd ch of turning ch-3. Ch 1, turn.

Row 5:
Sc in first sc; * sk next 3 sts, 7 trc in next sc; sk next 3 sts, sc in next st; rep from * across. Ch 1, turn.

Row 6:
Sc in first sc; * BPsc around each of next 7 trc; sc in next sc; rep from * across. Ch 3, turn.

Rep Rows 3 through 6 for desired length. At end of last row, do not ch 3; do not turn.

Finish off.

#63

Materials:
Yarn—One color

Instructions
Foundation ch: multiple of 3

Row 1 (right side):
Sc in 3rd ch from hook; * ch 4, working around post (see page 7) of sc just made, draw up 1/2" lp, YO, working around same post, draw up 1/2" lp, YO, draw through 3 lps on hook, YO and draw through 2 lps on hook; sk next 2 chs, sc in next ch; rep from * across. Ch 2, turn.

Row 2:
* Sc in next ch-4 sp, ch 4, working around post of sc just made, draw up 1/2" lp, YO, working around same post, draw up 1/2" lp, YO, draw through 3 lps on hook, YO and draw through 2 lps on hook; rep from * to beg 2 skipped chs; sc in 2nd ch of beg 2 skipped chs. Ch 2, turn.

Row 3:
* Sc in next ch-4 sp, ch 4, working around post of sc just made, draw up 1/2" lp, YO, working around same post, draw up 1/2" lp, YO, draw through 3 lps on hook, YO and draw through 2 lps on hook; rep from * to turning ch-2; sc in 2nd ch of turning ch-2. Ch 2, turn.

Rep Row 3 for desired length.

Last Row:
* Sc in next ch-4 sp, ch 2; rep from * to turning ch-2; dc in 2nd ch of turning ch-2.

Finish off.

#64

#65

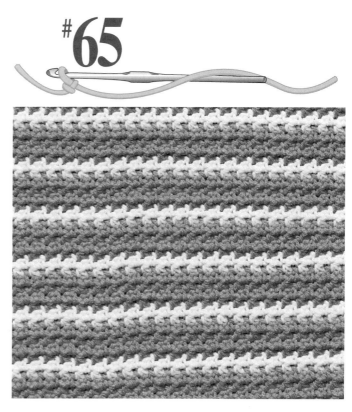

Materials:
Yarn—Color A **(dark)**; Color B **(light)**

Color Sequence:
2 rows Color A
2 rows Color B
end with 2 rows Color A

Instructions
Foundation ch with Color A: multiple of 7 + 6

Row 1 (right side):
Sc in 2nd ch from hook and in next ch, 3 sc in next ch; sc in next 2 chs; * sk next 2 chs, sc in next 2 chs, 3 sc in next ch; sc in next 2 chs; rep from * across. Ch 1, turn.

Row 2:
Sk first sc, working in BLs only, sc in next 2 sc, 3 sc in next sc; * sc in next 2 sc, sk next 2 sc, sc in next 2 sc, 3 sc in next sc; rep from * to last 3 sc; sc in next sc, sk next sc, sc in last sc. Change to Color B by drawing lp through; cut Color A. Ch 1, turn.

Working in color sequence, rep Row 2 for desired length. At end of last row, do not ch 1; do not turn.

Finish off.

Materials:
Yarn—Color A **(dark)**; Color B **(light)**

Color Sequence:
4 rows Color A
2 rows Color B
end with 4 rows Color A

Pattern Stitch

Cluster (CL):
Draw up lp in each of 2 sts indicated; YO and draw through all 3 lps on hook—CL made.

Instructions
Foundation ch: multiple of 2 + 1

Row 1 (right side):
CL (see Pattern Stitch) over 2nd ch from hook and in next ch; ch 1; * CL over next 2 chs; ch 1; rep from * across. Ch 1, turn.

Row 2:
CL over first ch-1 sp and first CL; ch 1; * CL over next ch-1 sp and next CL; ch 1; rep from * across. Ch 1, turn.

Note: *Change colors by drawing lp of new color through last lp of old color.*

Working in color sequence, rep Row 2 for desired length. At end of last row, do not ch 1; do not turn.

Finish off.

#66

Materials:
Yarn—One color

Pattern Stitch

Cluster (CL):
YO, draw up lp in st indicated, YO, draw through one lp on hook, YO, draw through 2 lps on hook; (YO, draw up lp in same st, YO, draw through one lp on hook, YO, draw through 2 lps on hook) twice; YO and draw through all 4 lps on hook—CL made.

Instructions

Foundation ch: multiple of 2

Row 1 (right side):
Sc in 2nd ch from hook and in each rem ch. Ch 2 (counts as first dc on following rows), turn.

Row 2:
CL (see Pattern Stitch) in next sc; * ch 1, sk next sc, CL in next sc; rep from * to last sc; ch 1, dc in last sc. Ch 2, turn.

Row 3:
* CL in next ch-1 sp; ch 1; rep from * to turning ch-2; dc in 2nd ch of turning ch-2. Ch 2, turn.

Rep Row 3 for desired length. At end of last row, do not ch 2; ch 1, turn.

Last Row:
Sc in each CL and in each ch to turning ch-2; sc in 2nd ch of turning ch-2.

Finish off.

#67

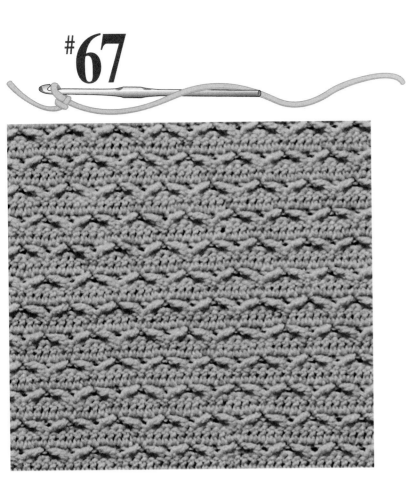

Materials:
Yarn—One color

Instructions
Foundation ch: multiple of 6 + 3

Row 1 (wrong side):
Dc in 3rd ch from hook **(2 skipped chs count as a dc)** and in each rem ch. Ch 2 **(counts as first dc on following rows)**, turn.

Row 2 (right side):
* Sk next 2 dc, trc in next dc, working behind trc just made, dc in 2 skipped dc; sk next dc, dc in next 2 dc, working in front of dc just made, trc in skipped dc; rep from ***** to beg 2 skipped chs; dc in 2nd ch of beg 2 skipped chs. Ch 2, turn.

Row 3:
Dc in each st to turning ch-2; dc in 2nd ch of turning ch-2. Ch 2, turn.

Row 4:
* Sk next dc, dc in next 2 dc, working in front of dc just made, trc in skipped dc; sk next 2 dc, trc in next dc, working behind trc just made, dc in 2 skipped dc; rep from ***** to turning ch-2; dc in 2nd ch of turning ch-2. Ch 2, turn.

Row 5:
Rep Row 3.

Row 6:
* Sk next 2 dc, trc in next dc, working behind trc just made, dc in 2 skipped dc; sk next dc, dc in next 2 dc, working in front of dc just made, trc in skipped dc; rep from ***** to turning ch-2; dc in 2nd ch of turning ch-2. Ch 2, turn.

Rep Rows 3 through 6 for desired length, ending with Row 5. At end of last row, do not ch 2; do not turn.

Finish off.

#68

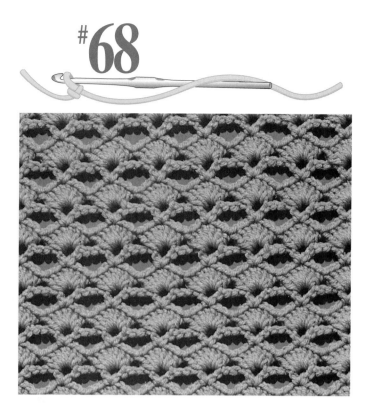

Materials:
Yarn—One color

Instructions

Foundation ch: multiple of 6 + 5

Row 1 (wrong side):
Dc in 5th ch from hook (beg 4 skipped chs count as a dc and a ch-2 sp); * ch 2, sk next 5 chs, in next ch work (dc, ch 2, dc)—V-st made; rep from * across. Turn.

Row 2 (right side):
SI st in ch-2 sp of first V-st; ch 2 (counts as first dc on this and following rows), 6 dc in same sp—beg shell made; sk next ch-2 sp; * 7 dc in ch-2 sp of next V-st—shell made; sk next ch-2 sp; rep from * to beg 4 skipped chs; 7 dc in sp formed by beg 4 skipped chs—shell made. Turn.

Row 3:
SI st in next 4 dc, ch 4 (counts as a dc and a ch-2 sp on this and following rows), dc in same dc as last sl st made—beg V-st made; * ch 2, in 4th dc of next shell work V-st; rep from * across. Turn.

Row 4:
SI st in ch-2 sp of first V-st, beg shell in same sp; * sk next ch-2 sp, in ch-2 sp of next V-st work shell; rep from * to beg V-st; shell in ch-2 sp of beg V-st. Turn.

Rep Rows 3 and 4 for desired length.

Finish off.

#69

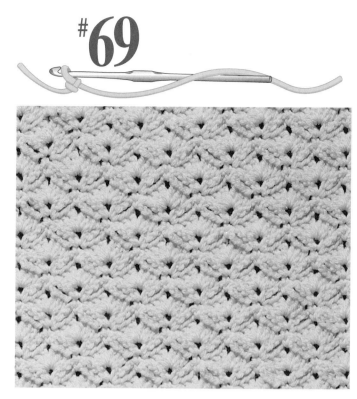

Materials:
Yarn—One color

Instructions

Foundation ch: multiple of 7 + 1

Row 1 (right side):
Sc in 2nd ch from hook and in each rem ch. Ch 1, turn.

Row 2:
Sc in first sc, (ch 3, sk next 2 sc, sc in next sc) twice; * ch 3, sc in next sc, (ch 3, sk next 2 sc, sc in next sc) twice; rep from * across. Ch 2 (counts as first dc on following rows), turn.

Row 3:
3 dc in next ch-3 sp; sc in next sc; * sk next ch-3 sp, in next ch-3 sp work (3 dc, ch 3, 3 dc)—shell made; sk next sc and next ch-3 sp, sc in next sc; rep from * to last ch-3 sp; 3 dc in last ch-3 sp; dc in last sc. Ch 1, turn.

Row 4:
Sc in first dc, ch 3, sk next 3 dc, in next sc work (sc, ch 3, sc)—V-st made; * ch 3, sc in ch-3 sp of next shell, ch 3, sk next 3 dc of same shell, in next sc work (sc, ch 3, sc)—V-st made; rep from * to last 4 sts; ch 3, sk next 3 dc, sc in 2nd ch of turning ch-2. Ch 1, turn.

Row 5:
Sc in first sc; ***** sk next ch-3 sp, in ch-3 sp of next V-st work shell; sk next sc and next ch-3 sp, sc in next sc; rep from ***** across. Ch 1, turn.

Row 6:
Sc in first sc, ch 3, sc in ch-3 sp of next shell, ch 3; ***** in next sc work V-st; ch 3, sc in ch-3 sp of next shell, ch 3; rep from ***** to last sc; sc in last sc. Ch 2, turn.

Row 7:
3 dc in next ch-3 sp; sc in next sc; ***** sk next ch-3 sp, in next ch-3 sp of next V-st work shell; sk next ch-3 sp, sc in next sc; rep from ***** to last ch-3 sp; 3 dc in last ch-3 sp; dc in last sc. Ch 1, turn.

Rep Rows 4 through 7 for desired length.

Last Row:
Sc in first 4 dc; ***** sk next sc, sc in next 3 dc, in next ch-3 sp, and in next 3 dc; rep from ***** to last 5 sts; sk next sc, sc in next 3 dc and in 2nd ch of turning ch-2.

Finish off.

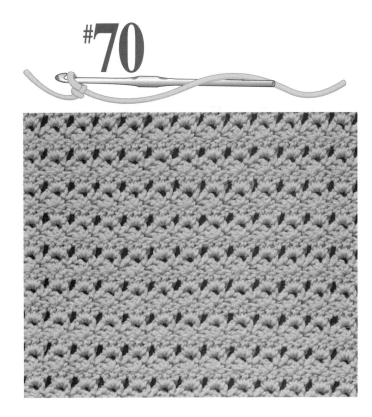

Materials:
Yarn—One color

Instructions
Foundation ch: multiple of 3 + 2

Row 1 (right side):
In 2nd ch from hook work (sc, ch 3, 2 dc)—shell made; ***** sk next 2 chs, in next ch work (sc, ch 3, 2 dc)—shell made; rep from ***** across. Ch 2, turn.

Row 2:
3 dc in ch-3 sp of each shell. Ch 1, turn.

Row 3:
In first dc work shell; in 2nd dc of each 3-dc group work shell; sc in 2nd ch of turning ch-2. Ch 2, turn.

Row 4:
3 dc in ch-3 sp of each shell. Ch 1, turn.

Rep Rows 3 and 4 for desired length. At end of last row, do not ch 1; do not turn.

Finish off.

#71

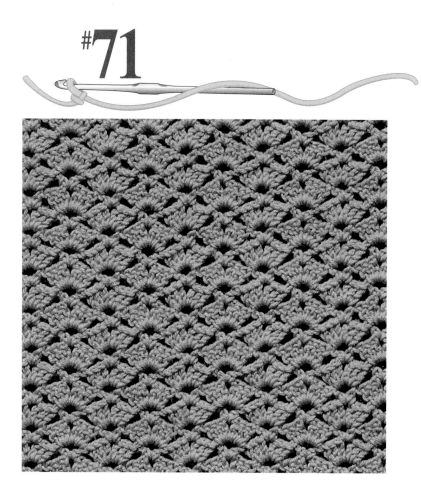

Materials:
Yarn—One color

Instructions

Foundation ch: multiple of 10 + 4

Row 1 (right side):
Dc in 4th ch from hook (3 skipped chs count as a dc and a ch-1 sp), sk next 4 chs, in next ch work (3 dc, ch 2, 3 dc)—shell made; * sk next 4 chs, in next ch work (dc, ch 2, dc)—V-st made; sk next 4 chs, in next ch work (3 dc, ch 2, 3 dc)—shell made; rep from * to last 5 chs; sk next 4 chs, in last ch work (dc, ch 1, dc). Ch 3 (counts as first dc and ch-1 sp on following rows), turn.

Row 2:
3 dc in next ch-1 sp; in ch-2 sp of next shell work V-st; * in ch-2 sp of next V-st work shell; in ch-2 sp of next shell work V-st; rep from * to beg 3 skipped chs; in sp formed by beg 3 skipped chs work (3 dc, ch 1, dc). Ch 3, turn.

Row 3:
Dc in next ch-1 sp, shell in ch-2 sp of next V-st; * V-st in ch-2 sp of next shell; shell in ch-2 sp of next V-st; rep from * to turning ch-3; in sp formed by turning ch-3 work (dc, ch 1, dc). Ch 3, turn.

Row 4:
3 dc in next ch-1 sp; V-st in next shell; * shell in next V-st; V-st in next shell; rep from * to turning ch-3; in sp formed by turning ch-3 work (3 dc, ch 1, dc). Ch 3, turn.

Rep Rows 3 and 4 for desired length. At end of last row, do not ch 3; do not turn.

Finish off.

#72

Materials:
Yarn—One color

Instructions

Foundation ch: multiple of 3 + 1

Row 1 (wrong side):
Sc in 2nd ch from hook and in each rem ch. Ch 1, turn.

Row 2 (right side):
Sc in each sc. Ch 2 (counts as first dc on following rows), turn.

Row 3:
3 dc in next sc; ch 2, turn; sc in 3rd dc of 3-dc group just made; ch 1, turn; 3 sc over ch-2 sp just made—puff made; * on working row, dc in next 2 sc, 3 dc in next sc; ch 2, turn; sc in 3rd dc of 3-dc group just made; ch 1, turn; 3 sc over ch-2 sp just made—puff made; rep from * to last sc; dc in last sc. Ch 1, turn.

Row 4:
Sc in first dc; * sk next 2 dc (below 3-sc of puff) working behind puff, sc in next dc (already used for sc of puff), sc in next 2 dc; rep from * across to last puff; sk next 2 dc (below 3-sc of puff); working behind last puff, sc in next dc (already used for sc of puff) and in 2nd ch of turning ch-2. Ch 1, turn.

Row 5:
Sc in each sc. Ch 1, turn.

Row 6:
Sc in each sc. Ch 2, turn.

Rep Rows 3 through 6 for desired length. At end of last row, do not ch 2; do not turn.

Finish off.

#73

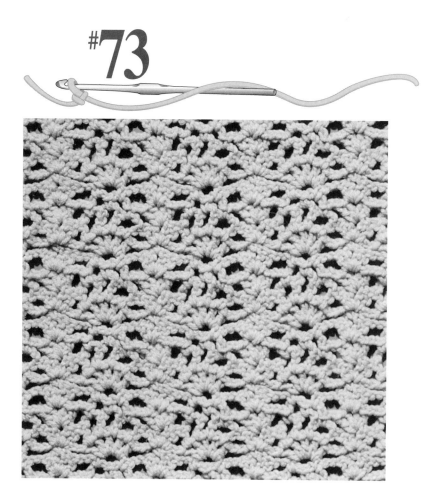

Materials:
Yarn—One color

Instructions
Foundation ch: multiple of 12 + 2

Row 1 (right side):
Sc in 2nd ch from hook; * ch 3, sk next 5 chs, in next ch work (dc, ch 1) 4 times; dc in same ch; ch 3, sk next 5 chs, sc in next ch; rep from * across. Ch 2 (counts as first dc on following rows), turn.

Row 2:
Dc in first sc, sk next ch-3 sp, (dc in next ch-1 sp, ch 3) 3 times; dc in next ch-1 sp, sk next ch-3 sp; * in next sc work (2 dc, ch 1, 2 dc); sk next ch-3 sp, (dc in next ch-1 sp, ch 3) 3 times; dc in next ch-1 sp, sk next ch-3 sp; rep from * to last sc; 2 dc in last sc. Ch 2, turn.

Row 3:
Dc in next dc, ch 2, sc in next ch-3 sp, (ch 3, sc in next ch-3 sp) twice; ch 2; * in next ch-1 sp work (2 dc, ch 1, 2 dc); ch 2, sc in next ch-3 sp, (ch 3, sc in next ch-3 sp) twice; ch 2; rep from * to last 3 sts; sk next dc, dc in next dc and in 2nd ch of turning ch-2. Ch 2, turn.

Row 4:
Dc in next dc, ch 2, sk next ch-2 sp, sc in next ch-3 sp, ch 3, sc in next ch-3 sp, ch 2; * sk next ch-2 sp, in next ch-1 sp work (2 dc, ch 1, 2 dc); ch 2, sk next ch-2 sp, sc in next ch-3 sp, ch 3, sc in next ch-3 sp, ch 2; rep from * to last 2 sts; dc in next dc and in 2nd ch of turning ch-2. Ch 1, turn.

Row 5:
Sc in first dc, ch 3, sk next ch-2 sp, in next ch-3 sp work (dc, ch 1) 4 times; dc in same sp; ch 3; * sk next ch-2 sp, sc in next ch-1 sp, ch 3, sk next ch-2 sp, in next ch-3 sp work (dc, ch 1) 4 times; dc in same sp; ch 3; rep from * to last 2 sts; sk next dc, sc in 2nd ch of turning ch-2. Ch 2, turn.

Rep Rows 2 through 5 for desired length, ending with Row 4. At end of last row, do not ch 1; do not turn.

Finish off.

#74

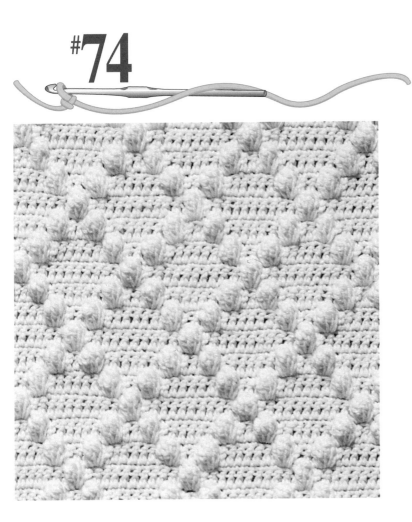

Materials:
Yarn—One color

Pattern Stitch

Bobble:
Keeping last lp of each trc on hook and working in front of sts on working row, 5 trc in ch-1 sp on 2nd row below; YO and draw through all 6 lps on hook—bobble made.

Instructions
Foundation ch: multiple of 12 + 6

Row 1 (right side):
Sc in 2nd ch from hook and in next ch; * ch 1, sk next ch, sc in next 11 chs; rep from * to last 3 chs; ch 1, sk next ch, sc in next 2 chs. Ch 2 (counts as first dc on following rows), turn.

Row 2:
Dc in next sc; * ch 1, sk next ch-1 sp, dc in next 11 sts; rep from * to last ch-1 sp; ch 1, sk last ch-1 sp, dc in last 2 sc. Ch 1, turn.

Row 3:
Sc in first 2 dc, bobble (see Pattern Stitch) in next ch-1 sp on 2nd row below; on working row, sc in next dc; * ch 1, sk next dc, sc in next 7 dc, ch 1, sk next dc, sc in next dc, bobble in next ch-1 sp on 2nd row below; on working row, sc in next dc; rep from * to turning ch-2; sc in 2nd ch of turning ch-2. Ch 2, turn.

Row 4:
Dc in next 3 sts; * ch 1, sk next ch-1 sp, dc in next 7 sts, ch 1, sk next ch-1 sp, dc in next 3 sts; rep from * to last sc; dc in last sc. Ch 1, turn.

Row 5:
Sc in first 4 dc; * bobble in next ch-1 sp on 2nd row below; on working row, sc in next dc, ch 1, sk next dc, sc in next 3 dc, ch 1, sk next dc, sc in next dc, bobble in next ch-1 sp on 2nd row below; on working row, sc in next 3 dc; rep from * to turning ch-2; sc in 2nd ch of turning ch-2. Ch 2, turn.

Row 6:
Dc in next 5 sts; * ch 1, sk next ch-1 sp, dc in next 3 sts, ch 1, sk next ch-1 sp, dc in next 7 sts; rep from * to last 2 ch-1 sps; ch 1, sk next ch-1 sp, dc in next 3 sts, ch 1, sk next ch-1 sp, dc in next 6 sts. Ch 1, turn.

continued

Row 7:
Sc in first 6 dc; * bobble in next ch-1 sp on 2nd row below; on working row, sc in next dc, ch 1, sk next dc, sc in next dc, bobble in next ch-1 sp on 2nd row below; on working row, sc in next 7 dc; rep from * to last 2 ch-1 sps on 2nd row below; bobble in next ch-1 sp on 2nd row below; on working row, sc in next dc, ch 1, sk next dc, sc in next dc, bobble in next ch-1 sp on 2nd row below; on working row, sc in next 5 dc and in 2nd ch of turning ch-2. Ch 2, turn.

Row 8:
Dc in next 7 sts, ch 1, sk next ch-1 sp; * dc in next 11 sts, ch 1, sk next ch-1 sp; rep from * to last 8 sts; dc in last 8 sts. Ch 1, turn.

Row 9:
Sc in first 6 dc, ch 1, sk next dc, sc in next dc; * bobble in next ch-1 sp on 2nd row below; on working row, sc in next dc, ch 1, sk next dc, sc in next 7 dc, ch 1, sk next dc, sc in next dc; rep from * to last ch-1 sp on 2nd row below; bobble in last ch-1 sp on 2nd row below; on working row, sc in next dc, ch 1, sk next dc, sc in next 5 dc and in 2nd ch of turning ch-2. Ch 2, turn.

Row 10:
Rep Row 6.

Row 11:
Sc in first 4 dc; * ch 1, sk next dc, sc in next dc, bobble in next ch-1 sp on 2nd row below; on working row, sc in next 3 dc, bobble in next ch-1 sp on 2nd row below; on working row, sc in next dc, ch 1, sk next dc, sc in next 3 dc; rep from * to turning ch-2; sc in 2nd ch of turning ch-2. Ch 2, turn.

Row 12:
Rep Row 4.

Row 13:
Sc in first 2 dc, ch 1, sk next dc, sc in next dc; * bobble in next ch-1 sp on 2nd row below; on working row, sc in next 7 dc, bobble in next ch-1 sp on 2nd row below; on working row, sc in next dc, ch 1, sk next dc, sc in next dc; rep from * to turning ch-2; sc in 2nd ch of turning ch-2. Ch 2, turn.

Row 14:
Rep Row 2.

Rep Rows 3 through 14 for desired length.

Last Row:
Sc in first 2 dc; * bobble in next ch-1 sp on 2nd row below; on working row, sc in next 11 dc; rep from * to last ch-1 sp on 2nd row below; bobble in last ch-1 sp on 2nd row below; on working row, sc in next dc and in 2nd ch of turning ch-2.

Finish off.

Materials:
Yarn—Color A (light); Color B (dark)

Pattern Stitches

Reverse Shell (rev shell):
Keeping last lp of each dc on hook, dc in same dc as last st made, in next 3 dc, in next sc, and in next 4 dc; YO and draw through all 10 lps on hook; ch 1—rev shell made.

Beginning Half Reverse Shell (beg half rev shell):
Keeping last lp of each dc on hook, dc in next 4 dc, YO and draw through all 5 lps on hook; ch 1—beg half rev shell made.

Half Reverse Shell (half rev shell):
Keeping last lp of each dc on hook, dc in same st as last dc made, in next 3 dc, and in next sc; YO and draw through all 6 lps on hook; ch 1—half rev shell made.

Instructions
Foundation ch with Color A: multiple of 8 + 2

Row 1 (right side):
Sc in 2nd ch from hook and in each rem ch. Ch 2 (counts as first dc on following rows), turn.

Row 2:
3 dc in first sc—beg half shell made; sk next 3 sc, sc in next sc; * sk next 3 sc, 7 dc in next sc—shell made;

sk next 3 sc, sc in next sc; rep from * to last 4 sc; sk next 3 sc, 4 dc in last sc—half shell made; change to Color B by drawing lp through; cut Color A. Ch 1, turn.

Row 3:
Sc in first dc; * ch 3, rev shell (see Pattern Stitches) over same dc as last sc made and in next 8 sts; ch 3, sc in same st as last dc made; rep from * across to last shell; ch 3, keeping last lp of each dc on hook, dc in same dc as last sc made, in next 7 sts, and in 2nd ch of turning ch-2; YO and draw through all 10 lps on hook; ch 1, pull tight—ending rev shell made; ch 3, sc in same ch as last dc made. Ch 1, turn.

Row 4:
Sc in first sc; * shell in top of next rev shell; sc in next sc; rep from * across; change to Color A by drawing lp through; cut Color B. Ch 2 (counts as first dc on following rows), turn.

Row 5:
Beg half rev shell (see Pattern Stitches) over next 4 dc; ch 3, sc in same st as last dc made; * ch 3, rev shell; ch 3, sc in same st as last dc made; rep from * to last 4 sts; ch 3, half rev shell over same st as last dc made, next 3 dc, and last sc. Ch 2, turn.

Row 6:
Beg half shell in top of next half rev shell; sc in next sc; * shell in top of next rev shell; sc in next sc; rep from * across to beg half rev shell; 4 dc in top of beg half rev shell; change to Color B by drawing lp through; cut Color A. Ch 1, turn.

Rep Rows 3 through 6 for desired length, ending with Row 5. At end of last row, do not ch 2. Ch 1, turn.

Last Row:
Sc in top of next half rev shell, in next 3 chs, in next sc, and in next 3 chs; * sc in top of next rev shell, in next 3 chs, in next sc, and in next 3 chs; rep from * across to beg half rev shell; sc in top of beg half rev shell.

Finish off.

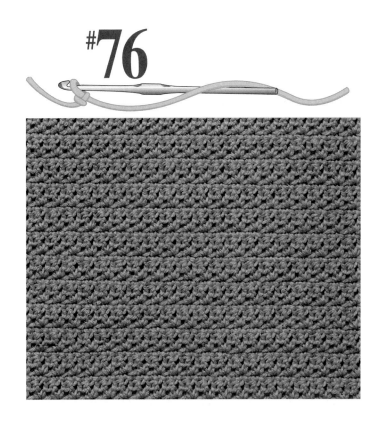

Materials:
Yarn—One color

Instructions
Foundation ch: multiple of 2

Row 1 (right side):
Sc in 2nd ch from hook and in each rem ch. Ch 2 (counts as first dc on following rows), turn.

Row 2:
Keeping last lp of each dc on hook, dc in first sc, sk next sc, dc in next sc, YO and draw through all 3 lps on hook; * ch 1, keeping last lp of each dc on hook, dc in same sc as last st made, sk next sc, dc in next dc, YO and draw through all 3 lps on hook; rep from * across; dc in same ch as last st made. Ch 1, turn.

Row 3:
Sc in each st and in each ch to turning ch-2; sc in 2nd ch of turning ch-2. Ch 2, turn.

Rep Rows 2 and 3 for desired length. At end of last row, do not ch 2; do not turn.

Finish off.

#77

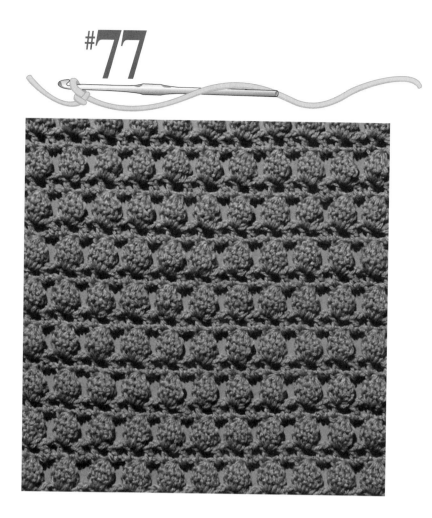

Materials:
Yarn—One color

Pattern Stitch

Cluster (CL):
Keeping last lp of each trc on hook, 5 trc in st indicated; YO and draw through all 6 lps on hook—CL made. Push CL to right side.

Instructions
Foundation ch: multiple of 4 + 2

Row 1 (wrong side):
Sc in 2nd ch from hook and in each rem ch.
Ch 3 (counts as first dc and ch-1 sp on following rows), turn.

Row 2 (right side):
Sk next sc, dc in next sc; * ch 1, sk next sc, dc in next sc; rep from * across. Ch 3, turn.

Row 3:
CL (see Pattern Stitch) in next dc; * ch 3, sk next dc, CL in next dc; rep from * to turning ch-3; ch 1, sk next ch of turning ch, dc in next ch. Ch 3, turn.

Row 4:
Dc in next CL, ch 1; * dc in next ch-3 sp, ch 1, dc in next CL, ch 1; rep from * to turning ch-3; sk next ch of turning ch, dc in next ch. Ch 3, turn.

Rep Rows 3 and 4 for desired length. At end of last row, do not ch 3. Ch 1, turn.

Last Row:
Sc in each dc and in each ch-1 sp to turning ch-3; sc in next 2 chs of turning ch-3.

Finish off.

#78

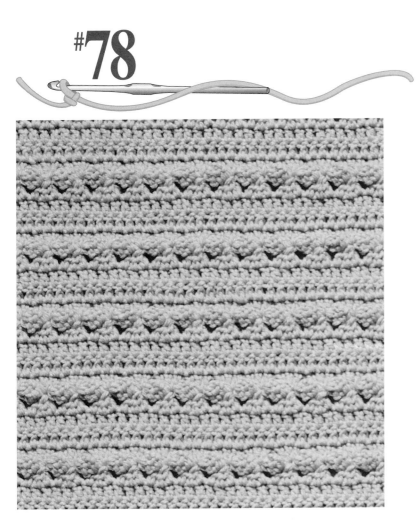

Materials:
Yarn—One color

Pattern Stitches

Cluster (CL):
Keeping last lp of each dc on hook, dc in next 3 sts; YO and draw through all 4 lps on hook—CL made.

2-Double Crochet Cluster (2-dc CL):
Ch 4, keeping last lp of each dc on hook, 2 dc in 4th ch from hook; YO and draw through all 3 lps on hook—2-dc CL made.

Instructions
Foundation ch: multiple of 3 + 2

Row 1 (wrong side):
CL (see Pattern Stitches) over 5th, 6th, and 7th chs from hook (beg 4 skipped chs count as a dc and a ch-2 sp); * 2-dc CL (see Pattern Stitches); CL over next 3 chs; rep from * to last ch; ch 2, dc in last ch. Ch 2, turn.

Row 2 (right side):
3 dc in next ch-2 sp; * sk next 2-dc CL, 3 dc in top of next CL; rep from * to beg 4 skipped chs; sk next 2 chs, dc in next ch. Ch 2 (counts as first dc on following rows), turn.

Row 3:
Dc in each dc to turning ch-2; dc in 2nd ch of turning ch-2. Ch 2, turn.

Row 4:
Dc in each dc to turning ch-2; dc in 2nd ch of turning ch-2. Ch 4 (counts as first dc and ch-2 sp on following rows), turn.

Row 5:
CL over next 3 dc; * 2-dc CL; CL over next 3 dc; rep from * to turning ch-2; ch 2, dc in 2nd ch of turning ch-2. Ch 2, turn.

Row 6:
3 dc in next ch-2 sp; * sk next 2-dc CL, 3 dc in top of next CL; rep from * to turning ch-4; sk next 2 chs of turning ch, dc in next ch. Ch 2, turn.

Rep Rows 3 through 6 for desired length. At end of last row, do not ch 2; do not turn.

Finish off.

#79

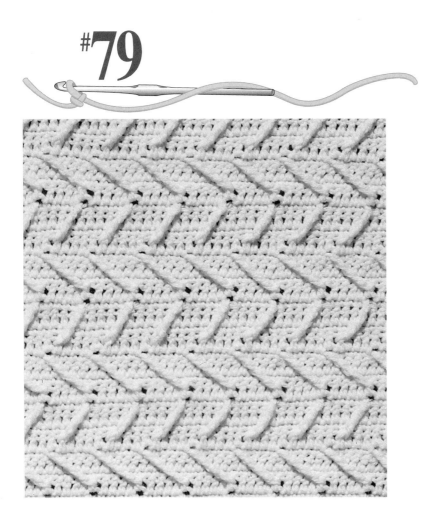

Materials:

Yarn—One color

Pattern Stitch

Front Post Triple Triple Crochet (FPtr trc):
YO 4 times, insert hook from front to back to front around post (see page 7) of st indicated, draw up lp, (YO, draw through 2 lps on hook) 5 times—FPtr trc made.

Instructions

Foundation ch: multiple of 5 + 4

Row 1 (right side):
Sc in 2nd ch from hook and in each rem ch.
Ch 2 (counts as first dc on following rows), turn.

Row 2:
Dc in each st. Ch 1, turn.

Row 3:
Sc in each dc to turning ch-2; sc in 2nd ch of turning ch-2. Ch 2, turn.

Row 4:
Rep Row 2.

Row 5:
Sc in first dc, FPtr trc (see Pattern Stitch) around post of 6th dc on 3rd row below; on working row, sk next dc, sc in next 4 dc; * on 3rd row below, sk next 4 dc, FPtr trc around post of next dc; on working row, sk next dc, sc in next 4 dc; rep from * to last 2 sts; sc in next dc and in 2nd ch of turning ch-2. Ch 2, turn.

Rows 6 and 7:
Rep Rows 2 and 3.

Row 8:
Rep Row 2.

Row 9:
Sc in first 6 dc, FPtr trc around post of 2nd dc on 3rd row below; on working row, sk next dc; * sc in next 4 dc; on 3rd row below, sk next 4 dc, FPtr trc around post of next dc; on working row, sk next dc; rep from * to turning ch-2; sc in 2nd ch of turning ch-2. Ch 2, turn.

Rep Rows 2 through 9 for desired length. At end of last row; do not ch 2. Ch 1, turn.

Last Row:
Sc in each st.

Finish off.

#80

Materials:
Yarn—Color A (dark); Color B (off white); Color C (light)

Instructions
Foundation ch with Color A: multiple of 12 + 4

Row 1 (right side):
Sc in 2nd ch from hook and in next 2 chs; * hdc in next 2 chs, dc in next 5 chs, hdc in next 2 chs, sc in next 3 chs; rep from * across. Ch 1, turn.

Row 2:
Sc in first 3 sc; * hdc in next 2 hdc, dc in next 5 dc, hdc in next 2 hdc, sc in next 3 sc; rep from * across; change to Color B by drawing lp through; cut Color A. Ch 1, turn.

Row 3:
Sc in each st; change to Color C by drawing lp through; cut Color B. Ch 2 (counts as first dc on following rows), turn.

Row 4:
Dc in next 3 sc, hdc in next 2 sc, sc in next 3 sc, hdc in next 2 sc; * dc in next 5 sc, hdc in next 2 sc, sc in next 3 sc, hdc in next 2 sc; rep from * to last 4 sc; dc in last 4 sc. Ch 2, turn.

Row 5:
Dc in next 3 dc, hdc in next 2 hdc, sc in next 3 sc, hdc in next 2 sc; * dc in next 5 dc, hdc in next 2 hdc, sc in next 3 sc, hdc in next 2 hdc; rep from * to last 4 sts; dc in next 3 dc and in 2nd ch of turning ch-2; change to Color B by drawing lp through; cut Color C. Ch 1, turn.

Row 6:
Sc in each st; change to Color A by drawing lp through; cut Color B. Ch 1, turn.

Row 7:
Sc in first 3 sc; * hdc in next 2 sc, dc in next 5 sc, hdc in next 2 sc, sc in next 3 sc; rep from * across. Ch 1, turn.

Row 8:
Sc in first 3 sc; * hdc in next 2 hdc, dc in next 5 dc, hdc in next 2 hdc, sc in next 3 sc; rep from * across; change to Color B by drawing lp through; cut Color A. Ch 1, turn.

Rep Rows 3 through 8 for desired length. At end of last row, do not ch 1; do not turn.

Finish off.

#81

Materials:
Yarn—One color

Pattern Stitches

Front Post Double Crochet (FPdc):
YO, insert hook from front to back to front around post (see page 7) of st indicated, draw up lp, (YO, draw through 2 lps on hook) twice—FPdc made.
Note: Sk st behind FPdc on working row.

Back Post Double Crochet (BPdc):
YO, insert hook from back to front to back around post (see page 7) of st indicated, draw up lp, (YO, draw through 2 lps on hook) twice—BPdc made.
Note: Sk st behind BPdc on working row.

Instructions
Foundation ch: multiple of 4

Row 1 (right side**):**
Dc in 3rd ch from hook (2 skipped chs counts as a dc) and in each rem ch. Ch 2 (counts as first dc on following rows), turn.

Row 2:
FPdc (see Pattern Stitches) around each of next 2 dc; BPdc (see Pattern Stitches) around next dc; * FPdc around each of next 3 dc; BPdc around next dc; rep from * to last 3 sts; FPdc around each of next 2 dc; dc in 2nd ch of beg 2 skipped chs. Ch 2, turn.

Row 3:
Dc in next 2 FPdc; * FPdc around next BPdc; dc in next 3 sts; rep from * across, working last dc in 2nd ch of turning ch-2. Ch 2, turn.

Row 4:
FPdc around each of next 2 dc; BPdc around next FPdc; * FPdc around each of next 3 dc; BPdc around next FPdc; rep from * to last 3 sts; FPdc around each of next 2 dc; dc in 2nd ch of turning ch-2. Ch 2, turn.

Rep Rows 3 and 4 for desired length, ending with Row 3. At end of last row, do not ch 2; do not turn.

Finish off.

#82

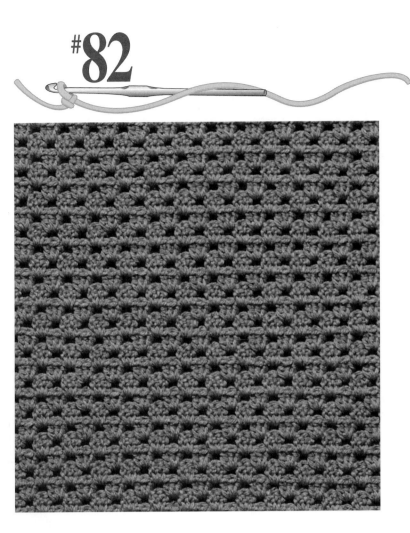

Materials:
Yarn—One color

Instructions
Foundation ch: multiple of 3

Row 1 (right side**):**
3 dc in 4th ch from hook **(**3 skipped chs count as a dc and a ch-1 sp**);** ✱ sk next 2 chs, 3 dc in next ch; rep from ✱ to last 2 chs; sk next ch, dc in last ch. Ch 2 **(**counts as first dc on following rows**),** turn.

Row 2:
2 dc between first dc and next 3-dc group; ✱ 3 dc between next two 3-dc groups; rep from ✱ to beg 3 skipped chs; 3 dc in sp formed by beg 3 skipped chs. Ch 2, turn.

Row 3:
✱ 3 dc between next two 3-dc groups; rep from ✱ to turning ch-2; dc in 2nd ch of turning ch-2. Ch 2, turn.

Row 4:
2 dc between first dc and next 3-dc group; ✱ 3 dc between next two 3-dc groups; rep from ✱ to turning ch-2; 3 dc in sp formed by turning ch-2. Ch 2, turn.

Rep Rows 3 and 4 for desired length. At end of last row, do not ch 2; do not turn.

Finish off.

#83

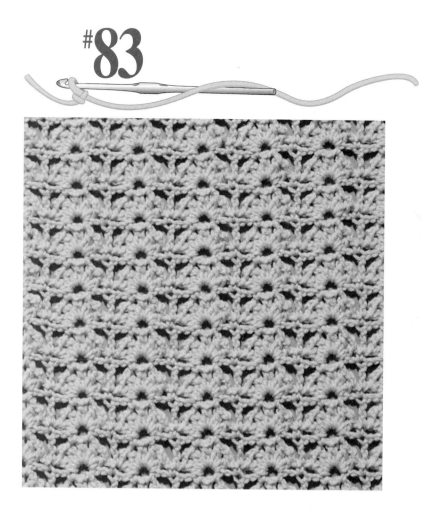

Materials:

Yarn—One color

Pattern Stitch

Cluster (CL):

Keeping last lp of each dc on hook, 2 dc in sp indicated; YO and draw through all 3 lps on hook—CL made.

Instructions

Foundation ch: multiple of 10 + 2

Row 1 (wrong side):

Sc in 2nd ch from hook; * ch 3, sk next 3 chs, sc in next ch, ch 3, sk next ch, sc in next ch, ch 3, sk next 3 chs, sc in next ch; rep from * across. Ch 1, turn.

Row 2 (right side):

Sc in first sc; * ch 1, sk next ch-3 sp, in next ch-3 sp work [CL (see Pattern Stitch), ch 2] 4 times; CL in same sp; ch 1, sk next sc, sc in next sc; rep from * across. Ch 5 (counts as first trc and ch-2 sp on following rows), turn.

Row 3:

Sk next ch-2 sp, (sc in next ch-2 sp, ch 2) twice; trc in next sc; * ch 2, sk next ch-2 sp, (sc in next ch-2 sp, ch 2) twice; trc in next sc; rep from * across. Ch 1, turn.

Row 4:

Sc in first trc, ch 1, sk next ch-2 sp, in next ch-2 sp work (CL, ch 2) 4 times; CL in same sp; ch 1; * sc in next trc, ch 1, sk next ch-2 sp, in next ch-2 sp work (CL, ch 2) 4 times; CL in same sp; ch 1; rep from * to turning ch-5; sk next 2 chs of turning ch, sc in next ch. Ch 5, turn.

Rep Rows 3 and 4 for desired length, ending with Row 3. At end of row, do not ch 1; do not turn.

Finish off.

#84

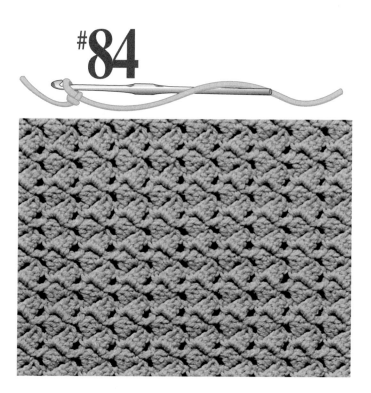

Materials:

Yarn—One color

Pattern Stitch

Cluster (CL):
Keeping last lp of each dc on hook, 3 dc in st or sp indicated; YO and draw through all 4 lps on hook—CL made.

Instructions

Foundation ch: multiple of 4 + 3

Row 1 (right side):
CL (see Pattern Stitch) in 4th ch from hook (beg 3 skipped chs count as a dc and a ch-1 sp); ch 1, sk next 2 chs, sc in next ch; * ch 3, CL in next ch; ch 1, sk next 2 chs, sc in next ch; rep from * across. Ch 3 (counts as first dc and ch-1 sp on following rows), turn.

Row 2:
* In next ch-3 sp work (sc, ch 3, CL, ch 1); rep from * to beg 3 skipped chs; sk next ch of beg 3 skipped chs, sc in next ch. Ch 3, turn.

Row 3:
* In next ch-3 sp work (sc, ch 3, CL, ch 1); rep from * to turning ch-3; sk next ch of turning ch, sc in next ch. Ch 3, turn.

Rep Row 3 for desired length. At end of last row, do not ch 3; do not turn.

Finish off.

#85

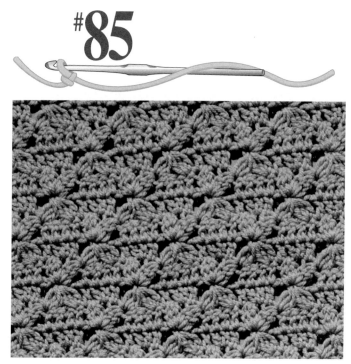

Materials:

Yarn—One color

Pattern Stitches

Cluster (CL):
Keeping last lp of each dc on hook, 3 dc in st indicated; sk next 2 sts, 3 dc in next st; YO and draw through all 7 lps on hook; ch 1—CL made.

3-Double Crochet Cluster (3-dc CL):
Keeping last lp of each dc on hook, 3 dc in sp indicated; YO and draw through all 4 lps on hook—3-dc CL made.

Instructions

Foundation ch: multiple of 8 + 5

Row 1 (right side):
Dc in 3rd ch from hook (2 skipped chs count as a dc) and in next 2 chs; * ch 2, CL (see Pattern Stitches) over next 4 chs; ch 2, dc in next 4 chs; rep from * across. Ch 2 (counts as first dc on following rows), turn.

Row 2:
Dc in next 3 dc, in ch-1 sp of next CL work [3-dc CL (see Pattern Stitches), ch 2, 3-dc CL]; * dc in next 4 dc, in ch-1 sp of next CL work (3-dc CL, ch 2, 3-dc CL); rep from * to last 4 sts; dc in next 3 dc and in 2nd ch of beg 2 skipped chs. Ch 3 (counts as first dc and ch-1 sp on following rows), turn.

continued

Row 3:

CL over first 4 dc; ch 2, dc in next 3-dc CL, in next 2 chs, and in next 3-dc CL; ch 2; ✳ CL over next 4 dc; ch 2, dc in next 3-dc CL, in next 2 chs, and in next 3-dc CL; ch 2; rep from ✳ to last 4 sts; CL over next 3 dc and 2nd ch of turning ch-2; ch 1, dc in same ch. Ch 2, turn.

Row 4:

In ch-1 sp of next CL work (3-dc CL, ch 2, 3-dc CL); ✳ sk next ch-2 sp, dc in next 4 dc, in ch-1 sp of next CL work (3-dc CL, ch 2, 3-dc CL); rep from ✳ to turning ch-3; sk next ch of turning ch, dc in next ch. Ch 2, turn.

Row 5:

Sk next 3-dc CL, dc in next 2 chs and in next 3-dc CL; ch 2, CL over next 4 dc; ch 2; ✳ dc in next 3-dc CL, in next 2 chs, and in next 3-dc CL; ch 2, CL over next 4 dc; ch 2; rep from ✳ to last 5 sts; dc in next 3-dc CL and in next 2 chs, sk next 3-dc CL, dc in 2nd ch of turning ch-2. Ch 2, turn.

Row 6:

Dc in next 3 dc, in ch-1 sp of next 6-dc CL work (3-dc CL, ch 2, 3-dc CL); ✳ dc in next 4 dc, in ch-1 sp of next CL work (3-dc CL, ch 2, 3-dc CL); rep from ✳ to last 4 sts; dc in next 3 dc and in 2nd ch of turning ch-2. Ch 3, turn.

Rep Rows 3 through 6 for desired length. At end of last row, do not ch 3; do not turn.

Finish off.

#86

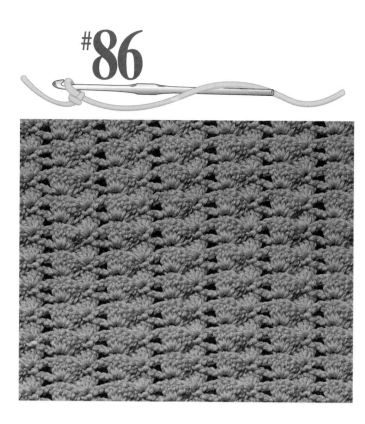

Materials:

Yarn—One color

Instructions

Foundation ch: multiple of 8 + 2

Row 1 (right side):

Sc in 2nd ch from hook; ✳ ch 2, sk next 3 chs, 5 dc in next ch; sk next 3 chs, sc in next ch; rep from ✳ across. Ch 2 (counts as first dc on following rows), turn.

Row 2:

3 dc in first sc; sk next 3 dc, sc in next dc, ch 2; ✳ 5 dc in next sc; sk next 3 dc, sc in next dc, ch 2; rep from ✳ to last sc; 2 dc in last sc. Ch 1, turn.

Row 3:

Sc in first dc, ch 2, 5 dc in next sc; sk next 3 dc; ✳ sc in next dc, ch 2, 5 dc in next sc; sk next 3 dc; rep from ✳ to turning ch-2; sc in 2nd ch of turning ch-2. Ch 2, turn.

Rep Rows 2 and 3 for desired length. At end of last row, do not ch 2; do not turn.

Finish off.

#87

Materials:
Yarn—One color

Pattern Stitches

Front Post Double Crochet (FPdc):
YO, insert hook from front to back to front around post (see page 7) of st indicated, draw up lp, (YO, draw through 2 lps on hook) twice—FPdc made.

Circle:
6 FPdc around next dc; turn piece upside down; 6 FPdc around prev dc on same row—circle made.

Instructions
Foundation ch: multiple of 10 + 1

Row 1 (right side):
Dc in 3rd ch from hook (2 skipped chs count as a dc) and in each rem ch. Ch 2 (counts as first dc on following rows), turn.

Row 2:
Dc in each dc to beg 2 skipped chs; dc in 2nd ch of beg 2 skipped chs. Ch 2, turn.

Row 3:
Dc in next 4 dc, work circle (see Pattern Stitches); * working behind circle, dc in top of same dc as beg part of circle made and in next 9 dc; work circle; rep from * to last 5 sts; dc in top of same dc as beg part of circle made, in next 3 dc, and in 2nd ch of turning ch-2. Ch 2, turn.

Row 4:
Dc in each st to turning ch-2; dc in 2nd ch of turning ch-2. Ch 2, turn.

Rows 5 and 6:
Rep Row 4.

Row 7:
Dc in next 9 dc, work circle; * working behind circle, dc in top of same dc as beg part of circle made and in next 9 dc; work circle; rep from * to last 10 sts; working behind circle, dc in top of same dc as beg part of circle made, in next 8 dc, and in 2nd ch of turning ch-2. Ch 2, turn.

Rows 8 through 10:
Rep Row 4.

Rep Rows 3 through 10 for desired length, ending with Row 4. At end of last row, do not ch 2; do not turn.

Finish off.

#88

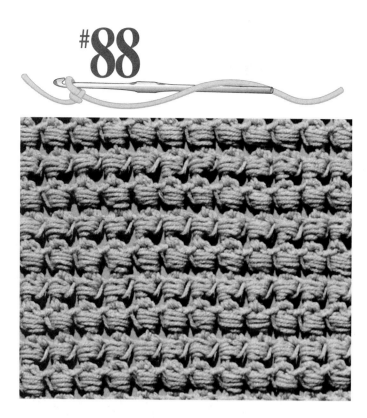

Materials:
Yarn—One color

Pattern Stitch

Puff Stitch (puff st):
YO, draw up lp around post **(see page 7)** of dc just made, **(**YO, draw up lp around post of same dc**)** 3 times; YO and draw through all 9 lps on hook; ch 1—puff st made.

Instructions
Foundation ch: multiple of 3

Row 1 (right side):
Dc in 4th ch from hook; * ch 2, puff st **(see Pattern Stitch)** around post of dc just made; sk next 2 chs, dc in next ch; rep from * to last 2 chs; ch 2, puff st around post of dc just made; sk next ch, dc in last ch. Ch 3, turn.

Row 2:
* Dc in next ch-2 sp, ch 2, puff st around post of dc just made; rep from * to beg 2 skipped chs; dc in 3rd ch of beg 3 skipped chs. Ch 3, turn.

Row 3:
* Dc in next ch-2 sp, ch 2, puff st around post of dc just made; rep from * to turning ch-3; dc in 3rd ch of turning ch-3. Ch 3, turn.

Rep Row 3 for desired length. At end of last row, do not ch 3; do not turn.

Finish off.

#89

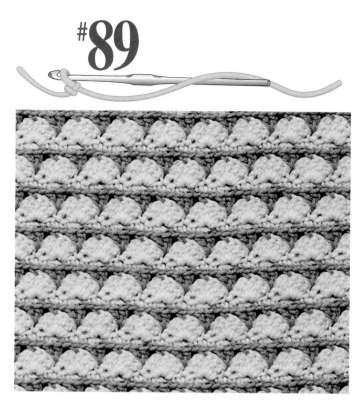

Materials:
Yarn—Color A **(light)**; Color B **(dark)**

Pattern Stitch

Cluster (CL):
(Draw up lp in BL of next dc**)** twice; YO and draw through all 3 lps on hook—CL made.

Instructions
Foundation ch with Color A: multiple of 6 + 2

Row 1 (wrong side):
Sc in 2nd ch from hook; * sk next 2 chs, 5 dc in next ch—shell made; sk next 2 chs, sc in next ch; rep from * across. Change to Color B by drawing lp through; drop Color A. Ch 3 (counts as first dc and ch-1 sp on following rows), turn.

Row 2 (right side):
Sc in 3rd dc of next shell, ch 1; * 2 dc in next sc; ch 1, sc in 3rd dc of next shell, ch 1; rep from * to last sc; dc in last sc. Finish off Color B. Do not turn.

Row 3:
With right side facing you and working in BLs only, with Color A at beg of prev row, sl st in next 2 chs; ch 1, sc in same ch as last sl st made; sc in next 3 sts; * CL (see Pattern Stitch) over next 2 dc; sc in next 3 sts; rep from * to last dc; sc in last dc. Ch 2 (counts as first dc on following rows), turn.

Row 4:

2 dc in first sc; sk next sc, sc in next sc, sk next sc; * 5 dc in next st; sk next sc, sc in next sc, sk next sc; rep from * to last sc; 3 dc in last sc. Change to Color B by drawing lp through; drop Color A. Ch 1, turn.

Row 5:

Sc in first dc, ch 1, 2 dc in next sc; ch 1; * sc in 3rd dc of next shell, ch 1, 2 dc in next sc; ch 1; rep from * to turning ch-2; sc in 2nd ch of turning ch-2. Finish off Color B. Do not turn.

Row 6:

With right side facing you and working in BLs only, draw up Color A in first sc of prev row; ch 1, sc in same sc and in next ch, CL over next 2 dc; * sc in next ch, in next sc, and in next ch; CL over next 2 dc; rep from * to last 2 sts; sc in next ch and in last sc. Ch 1, turn.

Row 7:

Sc in first sc, sk next sc, 5 dc in next sc; sk next sc, sc in next sc; * sk next sc, 5 dc in next sc; sk next sc, sc in next sc; rep from * across. Change to Color B by drawing lp through; drop Color A. Ch 3, turn.

Rep Rows 2 through 7 for desired length. At end of last row, do not ch 3; do not turn.

Finish off.

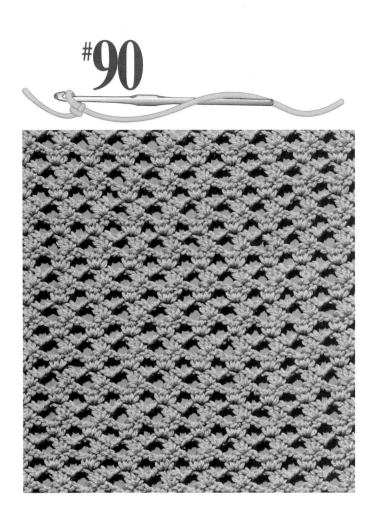

Materials:

Yarn—One color

Instructions

Foundation ch: multiple of 4 + 2

Row 1 (right side):

In 2nd ch from hook work (sc, 2 dc); * ch 2, sk next 3 chs, in next ch work (sc, 2 dc); rep from * to last 4 chs; sk next 3 chs, dc in last ch. Ch 1, turn.

Row 2:

In first dc work (sc, 2 dc); ch 2, sk next 2 dc, next sc, and next ch-2 sp; in next dc work (sc, 2 dc); * ch 2, sk next dc, next sc, and next ch-2 sp; in next dc work (sc, 2 dc); rep from * to last 2 sts; sk next dc, dc in last sc. Ch 1, turn.

Rep Row 2 for desired length. At end of last row, do not ch 1; do not turn.

Finish off.

#91

Materials:
Yarn—One color

Pattern Stitches

Front Post Double Crochet (FPdc):
YO, insert hook from front to back to front around post **(see page 7)** of st indicated, draw up lp, **(**YO, draw through 2 lps on hook**)** twice—FPdc made.
Note: Sk sc behind FPdc on working row.

Cable:
Ch 4, sl st around post **(see page 7)** of st indicated on 4th row below; with wrong side of ch-4 facing you, sc in top lp of each of next 4 chs—cable made.
Note: Sk sc behind cable on working row.

Instructions
Foundation ch: multiple of 9 + 8

Row 1 (right side)**:**
Sc in 2nd ch from hook and in each rem ch. Ch 1, turn.

Row 2:
Sc in each sc. Ch 1, turn.

Row 3:
Sc in first 2 sc, FPdc **(see Pattern Stitches)** around next sc on 2nd row below; on working row, sc in next sc; on 2nd row below, sk next sc, FPdc around next sc; **✱** on working row, sc in next 6 sc, FPdc around next sc on 2nd row below; on working row, sc in next sc; on 2nd row below, sk next sc, FPdc around next sc; rep from **✱** to last 2 sc; sc in last 2 sc. Ch 1, turn.

Row 4:
Sc in each st. Ch 1, turn.

Row 5:
Sc in first 2 sc, FPdc around next FPdc; on working row, sc in next sc, FPdc around next FPdc; on working row, sc in next 2 sc; **✱** on 4th row below, sk next 2 sc, cable **(see Pattern Stitches)** around post of next sc; on working row, sc in next 3 sc, FPdc around next FPdc; on working row, sc in next sc, FPdc around next FPdc; on working row, sc in next 2 sc; rep from **✱** across. Ch 1, turn.

Row 6:
Rep Row 4.

Row 7:
Sc in first 2 sc, FPdc around next FPdc; on working row, sc in next sc, FPdc around next FPdc; * on working row, sc in next 6 sc, FPdc around next FPdc; on working row, sc in next sc, FPdc around next FPdc; rep from * to last 2 sc; sc in last 2 sc. Ch 1, turn.

Row 8:
Rep Row 4.

Row 9:
Sc in first 2 sc, FPdc around next FPdc; on working row, sc in next sc, FPdc around next FPdc; on working row, sc in next 2 sc; * cable around post of next sc on 4th row below (under prev cable); on working row, sc in next 3 sc, FPdc around next FPdc; on working row, sc in next sc, FPdc around next FPdc; on working row, sc in next 2 sc; rep from * across. Ch 1, turn.

Row 10:
Rep Row 4.

Rep Rows 7 through 10 for desired length. At end of last row, do not ch 1; do not turn.

Finish off.

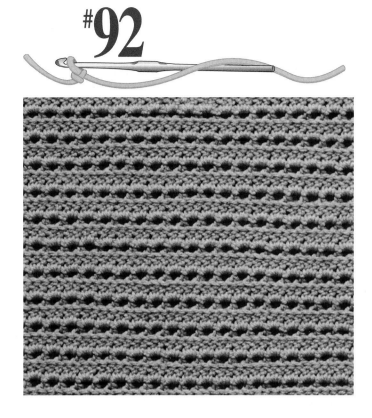

Materials:
Yarn—One color

Instructions
Foundation ch: multiple of 2 + 1

Row 1 (right side):
Hdc in 5th ch from hook (4 skipped chs count as a ch-1 sp, an hdc, and a ch-1 sp); * ch 1, sk next ch, hdc in next ch; rep from * across. Ch 2 (counts as first dc on following rows), turn.

Row 2:
2 dc in each ch-1 sp to beg 4 skipped chs; dc in each of next 2 chs of beg 4 skipped chs. Ch 3 (counts as first hdc and ch-1 sp on following rows), turn.

Row 3:
Sk next dc; * hdc in BL of next dc, ch 1, sk next dc; rep from * to turning ch-2; hdc in 2nd ch of turning ch-2. Ch 2, turn.

Row 4:
2 dc in each ch-1 sp to turning ch-3; dc in each of next 2 chs of turning ch-3. Ch 3, turn.

Rep Rows 3 and 4 for desired length. At end of last row, do not ch 3; do not turn.

Finish off.

#93

Materials:
Yarn—One color

Pattern Stitches

Puff Stitch (puff st):
YO, draw up lp in st indicated, (YO, draw up lp in same st) 4 times; YO, draw through 10 lps on hook; YO and draw through 2 lps on hook—puff st made. Push puff st to right side.

Front Post Double Crochet (FPdc):
YO, insert hook from front to back to front around post (see page 7) of next st on 2nd row below, (YO, draw through 2 lps on hook) twice—FPdc made.
Note: Sk st behind FPdc.

Instructions
Foundation ch: multiple of 12 + 8

Row 1 (right side):
Sc in 2nd ch from hook and in each rem sc. Ch 1, turn.

Row 2:
Sc in each sc. Ch 1, turn.

Row 3:
Sc in first 2 sc, FPdc (see Pattern Stitches) around post of next st on 2nd row below; on working row, sc in next sc, FPdc around post of next st on 2nd row

below; * on working row, sc in next 4 sc, puff st (see Pattern Stitches) in next sc; sc in next 4 sc, FPdc around post of next st on 2nd row below; on working row, sc in next sc, FPdc around post of next st on 2nd row below; rep from * to last 2 sc; sc in last 2 sc. Ch 1, turn.

Row 4:
Sc in each st. Ch 1, turn.

Row 5:
Sc in first 2 sc, FPdc around next FPdc; sc in next sc, FPdc around next FPdc; * sc in next 2 sc, puff st in next sc; sc in next 3 sc, puff st in next sc; sc in next 2 sc, FPdc around next FPdc; sc in next sc, FPdc around next FPdc; rep from * to last 2 sc; sc in last 2 sc. Ch 1, turn.

Row 6:
Rep Row 4.

Row 7:
Sc in first 2 sc, FPdc around next FPdc; sc in next sc, FPdc around next FPdc; * sc in next 4 sc, puff st in next sc; sc in next 4 sc, FPdc around next FPdc; sc in next sc, FPdc around next FPdc; rep from * to last 2 sc; sc in last 2 sc. Ch 1, turn.

Row 8:
Rep Row 4.

Row 9:
Sc in first 2 sc, FPdc around next FPdc; sc in next sc, FPdc around next FPdc; * sc in next 9 sc, FPdc around next FPdc; sc in next sc, FPdc around next FPdc; rep from * to last 2 sc; sc in last 2 sc. Ch 1, turn.

Row 10:
Rep Row 4.

Rep Rows 3 through 10 for desired length. At end of last row, do not ch 1; do not turn.

Finish off.

#94

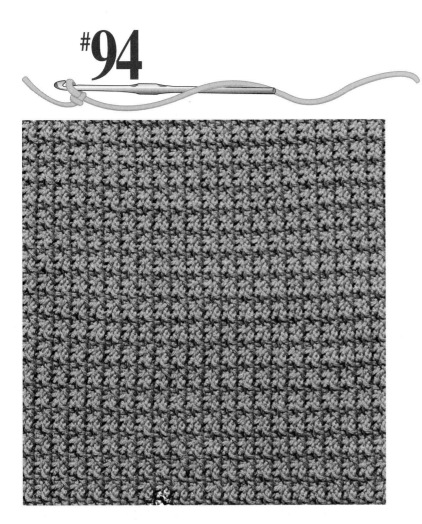

Materials:
Yarn—One color

Pattern Stitches

Back Post Double Crochet (BPdc):
YO, insert hook from back to front to back around post (see page 7) of st indicated, draw up lp, (YO, draw through 2 lps on hook) twice—BPdc made.

Front Post Double Crochet (FPdc):
YO, insert hook from front to back to front around post (see page 7) of st indicated, draw up lp, (YO, draw through 2 lps on hook) twice—FPdc made.

Instructions
Foundation ch: multiple of 2

Row 1 (right side):
Dc in 3rd ch from hook (2 skipped chs count as an hdc), hdc in next ch; * dc in next ch, hdc in next ch; rep from * across. Ch 2 (counts as first hdc on following rows), turn.

Row 2:
* BPdc (see Pattern Stitches) around next dc; hdc in next hdc; rep from * across, working last hdc in 2nd ch of beg 2 skipped chs. Ch 2, turn.

Row 3:
* FPdc (see Pattern Stitches) around next BPdc; hdc in next hdc; rep from * across, working last hdc in 2nd ch of turning ch-2. Ch 2, turn.

Row 4:
* BPdc around next FPdc; hdc in next hdc; rep from * across, working last hdc in 2nd ch of turning ch-2. Ch 2, turn.

Rep Rows 3 and 4 for desired length. At end of last row, do not ch 2; do not turn.

Finish off.

#95

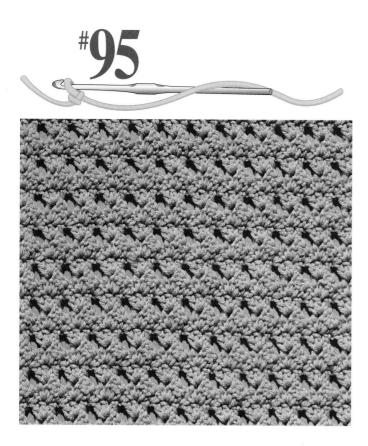

Materials:

Yarn—One color

Instructions

Foundation ch: multiple of 3 + 2

Row 1 (wrong side):
In 2nd ch from hook work (sc, ch 3, 2 dc)—shell made;
* sc in next ch, sk next ch, in next ch work (sc, ch 3,
2 dc)—shell made; rep from * across. Ch 2 (counts as
first dc on following rows), turn.

Row 2 (right side):
Dc in next dc and in next ch-3 sp, 3 dc in ch-3 sp of
each shell. Ch 1, turn.

Row 3:
In first dc work (sc, ch 3, 2 dc)—shell made; sk next dc;
* sc in next dc, sk next dc, in next dc work (sc, ch 3,
2 dc)—shell made; rep from * across. Ch 2, turn,
leaving turning ch-2 unworked.

Rep Rows 2 and 3 for desired length, ending with
Row 2. At end of last row, do not ch 1; do not turn.

Finish off.

#96

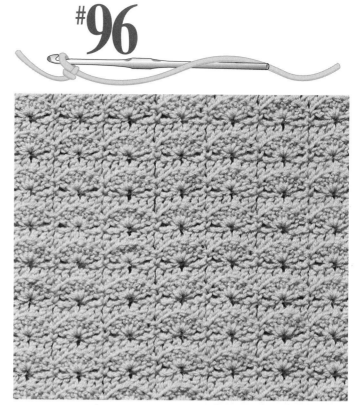

Materials:

Yarn—One color

Instructions

Foundation ch: multiple of 6 + 2

Row 1 (wrong side):
Sc in 2nd ch from hook, sk next 2 chs, 6 dc in next ch;
* sk next 2 chs, sc in next ch, sk next 2 chs, 6 dc in next
ch; rep from * to last 3 chs; sk next 2 chs, sc in last ch.
Ch 2 (counts as first dc on following rows), turn.

Row 2 (right side):
Working in BLs only, dc in next 3 dc, ch 1, dc in next
3 dc; * ch 1, sk next sc, dc in next 3 dc, ch 1, dc in next
3 dc; rep from * to last sc; dc in last sc. Ch 1, turn.

Row 3:
Sc in first dc, sk next 3 dc, 6 dc in next ch; sk next 3 dc;
* sc in next ch, sk next 3 dc, 6 dc in next ch; sk next
3 dc; rep from * to turning ch-2; sc in 2nd ch of turning
ch-2. Ch 2, turn.

Rep Rows 2 and 3 for desired length. At end of last
row, do not ch 2; do not turn.

Finish off.

#97

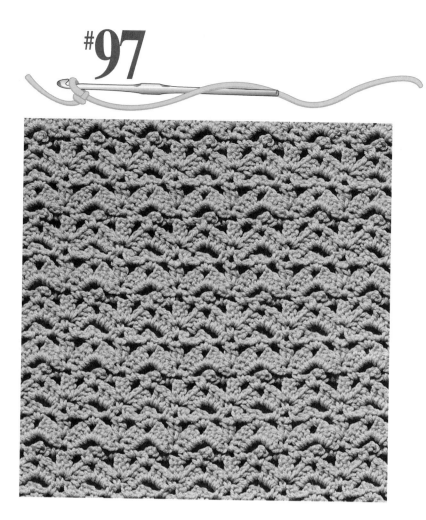

Materials:
Yarn—One color

Instructions
Foundation ch: multiple of 7 + 3

Row 1 (right side):
Dc in 3rd ch from hook (2 skipped chs count as first dc); * ch 2, sk next 2 chs, in next ch work (sc, ch 3, sl st in 3rd ch from hook—picot made; sc); ch 2, sk next 2 chs, dc in next 2 chs; rep from * across. Ch 1, turn.

Row 2:
Sc in first dc, sk next dc, sc in next ch-2 sp, ch 6, sk next picot, sc in next ch-2 sp; * ch 1, sk next 2 dc, sc in next ch-2 sp, ch 6, sk next picot, sc in next ch-2 sp; rep from * to last 2 sts; sk next dc, sc in 2nd ch of beg 2 skipped chs. Ch 1, turn.

Row 3:
Sc in first sc, in next ch-6 sp work (3 dc, ch 2, 3 dc)—shell made; * sc in next ch-1 sp; in next ch-6 sp work (3 dc, ch 2, 3 dc)—shell made; rep from * to last 2 sc; sk next sc, sc in last sc. Ch 2, turn.

Row 4:
Dc in first sc; * ch 2, in ch-2 sp of next shell work (sc, picot, sc); ch 2, 2 dc in next sc; rep from * across. Ch 1, turn.

Row 5:
Sc in first dc, sk next dc, sc in next ch-2 sp, ch 6, sk next picot, sc in next ch-2 sp; * ch 1, sk next 2 dc, sc in next ch-2 sp, ch 6, sk next picot, sc in next ch-2 sp; rep from * to last 2 sts; sk next dc, sc in 2nd ch of turning ch-2. Ch 1, turn.

Rep Rows 3 through 5 for desired length. At end of last row, do not ch 1; do not turn.

Finish off.

#98

Materials:
Yarn—One color

Pattern Stitch

Blackberry (BB):
Draw up lp in next sc, (YO, draw through last lp on hook) 3 times; keeping ch-3 just made to front of work, YO and draw through both lps on hook— BB made.

Instructions
Foundation ch: multiple of 2 + 1

Row 1 (wrong side):
Sc in 2nd ch from hook and in each rem ch. Ch 1, turn.

Row 2 (right side):
Sc in first sc; * BB (see Pattern Stitch) in next sc; sc in next sc; rep from * to last sc; sc in last sc. Ch 1, turn.

Row 3:
Sc in each st. Ch 1, turn.

Row 4:
Sc in first 2 sc; * BB in next sc; sc in next sc; rep from * across. Ch 1, turn.

Row 5:
Rep Row 3.

Rep Rows 2 through 5 for desired length. At end of last row, do not ch 1; do not turn.

Finish off.

#99

Material:
Yarn—One color

Instructions
Foundation ch: multiple of 6

Row 1 (right side):
Dc in 3rd ch from hook (2 skipped chs count as a dc); * in next ch work (2 dc, ch 1, 2 dc); YO, draw up lp in next ch, YO, draw through 2 lps on hook; YO, sk next 3 chs, draw up lp in next ch, (YO, draw through 2 lps on hook) 3 times; rep from * to last 3 chs; in next ch work (2 dc, ch 1, 2 dc); dc in last 2 chs. Ch 2 (counts as first dc on following rows), turn.

Row 2:
Dc in next dc, sk next 2 dc; * in next ch-1 sp work (2 dc, ch 1, 2 dc); YO, draw up lp in next dc, YO, draw through 2 lps on hook; YO, sk next 3 sts, draw up lp in next dc, (YO, draw through 2 lps on hook) 3 times; rep from * to last ch-1 sp; in last ch-1 sp work (2 dc, ch 1, 2 dc); sk next 2 dc, dc in next dc and in 2nd ch of beg 2 skipped chs. Ch 2, turn.

Row 3:
Dc in next dc, sk next 2 dc; * in next ch-1 sp work (2 dc, ch 1, 2 dc); YO, draw up lp in next dc, YO, draw through 2 lps on hook; YO, sk next 3 sts, draw up lp in next dc, (YO, draw through 2 lps on hook) 3 times; rep from * to last ch-1 sp; in last ch-1 sp work (2 dc, ch 1, 2 dc); sk next 2 dc, dc in next dc and in 2nd ch of turning ch-2. Ch 2, turn.

Rep Row 3 for desired length. At end of last row, do not ch 3; do not turn.

Finish off.

#100

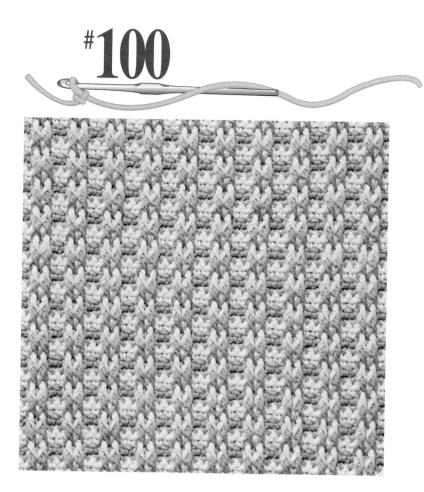

Materials:
Yarn—Color A **(light)**; Color B **(dark)**

Color Sequence:
2 rows Color A
2 rows Color B
end with 2 rows Color A

Pattern Stitch

Front Post Double Crochet (FPdc):
YO, insert hook from front to back to front around post **(see page 7)** of st indicated, **(**YO, draw through 2 lps on hook**)** twice—FPdc made.

Instructions
Foundation ch with Color A: multiple of 4 + 3

Row 1 (wrong side):
Sc in 2nd ch from hook and in each rem ch. Change to Color B by drawing lp through; cut Color A. Ch 1, turn.

Row 2 (right side):
Sc in each sc. Ch 1, turn.

Row 3:
Rep Row 2. At end of row, change to Color A by drawing lp through; cut Color B. Ch 1, turn.

Row 4:
Sc in first 2 sc; on 3rd row below, sk first 2 sc, FPdc (see Pattern Stitch) around each of next 2 sc; on working row, sk next 2 sc, sc in next 2 sc; * on 3rd row below, sk next 2 sc, FPdc around each of next 2 sc; on working row, sk next 2 sc, sc in next 2 sc; rep from * across. Ch 1, turn.

Row 5:
Sc in each sc and in each FPdc. Change to Color B by drawing lp through; cut Color A. Ch 1, turn.

Row 6:
Sc in first 2 sc; * on 2nd row below, FPdc around each of next 2 FPdc; on working row, sk next 2 sc, sc in next 2 sc; rep from * across. Ch 1, turn.

Row 7:
Sc in each sc and in each FPdc. Change to next color in sequence by drawing lp through; cut prev color. Ch 1, turn.

Rep Rows 6 and 7 for desired length. At end of last row, do not ch 1; do not turn.

Finish off.

#101

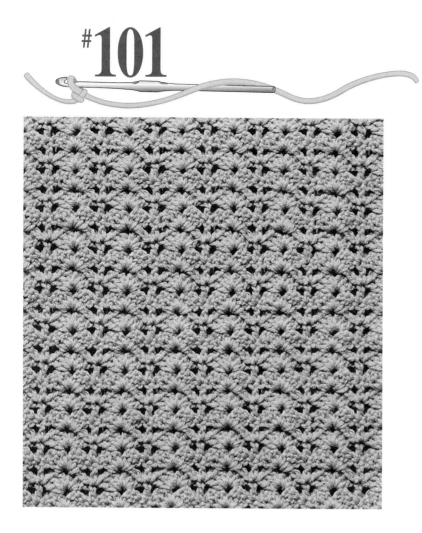

Materials:
Yarn—One color

Instructions
Foundation ch: multiple of 6 + 2

Row 1 (right side):
Sc in 2nd ch from hook and in each rem ch.
Ch 2 (counts as first dc on following rows), turn.

Row 2:
* Sk next 2 sc, in next sc work (3 dc, ch 2, 3 dc)—shell made; sk next 2 sc, dc in next sc; rep from * across. Ch 2, turn.

Row 3:
In ch-2 sp of next shell work shell; sk next 3 dc of same shell; * dc in next dc, in ch-2 sp of next shell work shell; sk next 3 dc of same shell; rep from * to turning ch-2; dc in 2nd ch of turning ch-2. Ch 2, turn.

Rep Row 3 for desired length. At end of last row, do not ch 2. Ch 1, turn.

Last Row:
Sc in first dc, sk next dc, sc in next 2 dc, in next ch-2 sp, and in next 2 dc; sk next dc; * sc in next dc, sk next dc, sc in next 2 dc, in next ch-2 sp, and in next 2 dc; sk next dc; rep from * to turning ch-2; sc in 2nd ch of turning ch-2.

Finish off.